Building

Design

Portfolios

ROCKPORT

Building

Design

Portfolios

GLOUCESTER MASSACHUSETTS

ROCKPORT
PUBLISHERS

Innovative Concepts for Presenting Your Work

Sara Eisenman

First published in the United States of America by
Rockport Publishers, a member of
Quayside Publishing Group
100 Cummings Center
Suite 406-L
Beverly, Massachusetts 01915-6101
Telephone: (978) 282-9590
Fax: (978) 283-2742
www.rockpub.com

Library of Congress Cataloging-in-Publication Data
Eisenman, Sara.
   Building design portfolios : innovative concepts for present-
ing your work / Sara Eisenman.
      p.   cm.
   Includes bibliographical references and index.
   ISBN 1-59253-223-3 (hardback)
   1. Art portfolios—Design. 2. Graphic arts—Marketing. 3.
Design services—Marketing. I. Title.

  NC1001.E48 2006
  741.6068'8—dc22   2005030865
                                   CIP

ISBN-13: 978-1-59253-438-8
ISBN-10: 1-59253-438-4

10 9 8 7 6 5 4 3

Design: Sara Eisenman
Layout and Production: Carol Petro
Cover Design: Sara Eisenman
Photography: Allan Penn Photography
Portfolio Icon: Isaac Tobin

Printed in China

To the two best pages in my portfolio,

Addison and Madeline

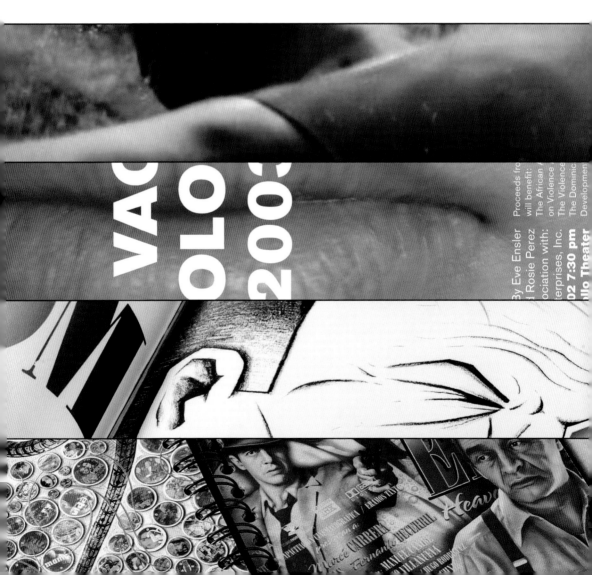

contents

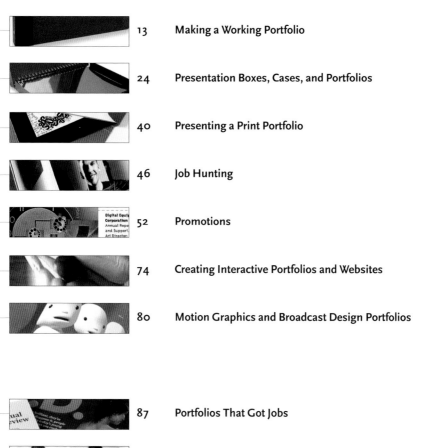

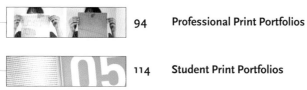

Introduction

By definition, a design portfolio is a grouping of loose sheets collected in a portable case. But today, portfolios assume a range of new forms: websites, motion portfolios, files on disc, portable document format (PDF), and limited-edition books or monographs. Despite their differences, these presentation forms share a surprising number of similarities.

Let's take a brief look at the history of design portfolios. Before and well into the twentieth century, designers were most often employed by printers, acting as in-house designers for all kinds of printed information, including invitations, manuals, books, or advertisements. In these cases, the portfolio usually took the form of a type specimen book, where previously printed samples showed how a specific typeface, ornament, dingbat, and border worked on the page.

Among the earliest examples of type specimen sheets is Trissino's display of Arrighi's italic, circa 1526. Also worth noting are the lovely eighteenth-century Fournier and Bodoni specimen books, which display both typefaces and ornaments offered by the printers to their customers. There's also the long and distinguished series of printers' manuals from Johannes Enschedé of Haarlem, the Netherlands, displaying the rich variety of typefaces produced by this foundry from the sixteenth century through the twentieth century.

In nineteenth-century America, most printers issued elaborate and extensive type specimen books, with the most thorough and interesting coming from the Bruce Type Foundry. Other examples include the celebrated Harpel specimen book from Cincinnati, and the long succession of elaborate American Type Founders type specimen books that displayed the myriad typefaces and borders offered by that enormous foundry. Clients could review type designs and faces in various sizes and weights and familiarize themselves with the house design style specific to that printer or type shop. Naturally, the different shops were very distinctive.

By the early twentieth century, designers began to operate independently of printers. Sir Francis Meynell, who conceived and directed England's Nonesuch Press, saw himself as an architect rather than a builder, a specifier rather than a printer. Rather than contracting printing locally, he went to extraordinary efforts to use the best printers throughout the world, regardless of cost or inconvenience. During this period, publishing companies and food and product manufacturers began to hire staff designers. Governments also hired designers to design money as well as postage stamps. If staff designers were not able or available to design products, the service was "jobbed out" to highly respected artists and engravers.

By the middle of the twentieth century, the art departments of several universities and colleges began offering graphic design courses, where students learned from teachers in classroom settings, rather than through apprenticeships. At this time, a portfolio, or a carried case similar to

OPPOSITE **Designer: Skolos-Wedell**

those that architects produce, became a routine appendage for any aspiring student. For many years, the black leather carrying case with interior ring binder and vinyl sleeves or black pages was the preferred portfolio style. But since the 1950s, popular presentation styles have evolved from samples mounted on fancy felt-backed boards to websites accompanied by loosely assembled samples in personalized presentation boxes. Nowadays, a number of designers even favor electronic files, often in PDFs, which they disseminate over the Internet.

Still, certain elements of presentation remain reasonably consistent when job hunting. If you are seeking advice on how to write and design good résumés and cover letters or how to assemble and design portfolios, presentation boxes, and websites, you will find it here. You'll also discover the best ways to present yourself as a competent problem solver and talented designer. In putting this book together, deciding the order of the table of contents was a challenge, in large part because websites are such a popular presentation form that it's tempting to discuss them first. "Send me your URL" is fast becoming a more common request than "bring in your portfolio." But according to many design leaders, a website is generally considered an introduction—a preview to the print portfolio that will follow. As a result, chapter one starts with the basics of a working portfolio, and interactive portfolios and websites are covered in chapter six.

Following these trends, preferences, and expectations, many schools now suggest that students offer a wide range of materials in their print portfolios, from traditional printed samples to DVDs featuring motion design. Students also are frequently advised to design a website during their studies, or shortly after graduating, in order to promote themselves as both print designers and website designers. In time, as a designer becomes established, a website becomes an important tool for generating work. But to most employers, the person remains the critical element, the problem solver behind the concept. Great work done in school or college is not a complete representation of the designer to come. Often, the assignments and problems the students have been asked to solve include very sophisticated subjects and texts, giving the work a polished, urbane look. An art director wants and needs to be assured that the new employee can produce the same caliber of work when designing all kinds of materials, from commercial book covers to text-heavy advertisements. In addition, when seeking an in-house employee, an employer is always looking for someone who will fit well into the existing work environment and integrate comfortably with the staff.

This book also strives to show you the best way to display your talent. Because fads and fashions are fleeting, and the leather case or aluminum portfolio that's popular now may not be always be available, I have chosen to show only a few portfolios and boxes currently available in art stores. Ultimately, a portfolio is not about the carrying case but, rather, about the work you show, "the gathering of loose sheets collected in a portable case." Many designers featured in this book asked me if I wanted to show their portfolio case or the designs inside. My answer was always both, and for this reason, you are invited to review some truly extraordinary student and professional design work inside the portable case.

As you will see in the gallery of portfolios, there are as many ways to approach portfolio presen-

OPPOSITE **Designer: Jim Drobka**

tation as there are designers. Using the variety of opinions, examples, and guidelines presented in this book, you will be better equipped to make informed decisions when creating a portfolio of your work.

There is no perfect presentation, as shown by the wide variety of perspectives and solutions in this book. Still, there are elements in the vast array of portfolios that are consistent. Remember that a résumé is extremely important as your fore-runner; it should be created as a sample of basic information design. In addition, all the pieces of a presentation you choose to include, such as your business card, résumé, CD, packaging, or promotional materials, should be coordinated and consistent down to the typeface you select. Everything must be clean, neat, and fresh, and give plenty of thought to the sequence and organization of samples, as well as the variety of work shown.

In general, print portfolios are still the best method for young designers to secure jobs, since live presentation is naturally part of that process. Websites as portfolios are effective for work that cannot be easily viewed in printed form, such as Flash elements, interactive com-ponents, or actual website design. For estab-lished designers, websites and PDFs are rapidly becoming the most logical means of advertising; some designers feel that PDFs are as effective as websites.

The most important thing to understand is that self promotion, while important, should not take up every waking moment, nor should it look like it took most of your time. It should not be so elaborate that it outshines the work you are exhibiting, nor should it be self-indulgent. It need not use the most expensive products avail-able, but it should be more creative than most off-the-shelf solutions. In the end, the perfectly designed system for displaying your talent will reflect you, your interests, your design skills, and your unique creativity.

PART I

The Components of a Great Portfolio

Making a
Working Portfolio

What are the first decisions you'll face when planning your portfolio? How should you approach those choices? Depending on your design training, it is possible that you already have formed some ideas or received guidance or advice. Maybe you have seen presentation boxes you like in the art store, or perhaps another student or designer created a portfolio that has influenced you.

One way to begin is to remember that this is just one portfolio; you can redesign it next year or next week. Knowing this can make any big project less intimidating. There is no best way to design your portfolio. Instead, approach it as a design project where you are the subject. It's also important to consider the audience you expect to address. Do you intend to show your portfolio to corporate decision makers, advertising creative directors, publishers, museums directors, or merchants? Does the presentation need to be distinctive to show off your strengths? No matter how you answer these questions, one of the most important things to recognize is that the container is secondary to the content. It shouldn't be so fussy or pretentious that it overpowers your work. And what's in the container should be an assemblage; a grouping of design pieces that composes a cohesive, unified whole.

For recent graduates, design work generally addresses problems they were asked to solve in class, and those samples inevitably reflect the influence of specific teachers. The danger is that an art director may review several portfolios with similar work, making it difficult to distinguish between applicants from the same school. Consider designing extra pieces to help your portfolio stand out. Completing an internship is also a good strategy for producing professional work in a specific area. If your dream is to work in an advertising agency, for example, an internship at a reputable firm is likely to provide both valuable portfolio material and professional experience.

Another good strategy is to take the time to create samples in your area of interest. If you hope to design book jackets, for example, you can redesign the covers of several well-known books. It's a good idea to use literary classics, because most viewers are familiar with the content, making it easier to judge your design solution. This kind of extra effort demonstrates enthusiasm and initiative. It also produces solid portfolio pieces and shows how you would solve a specific type of problem. One important piece of advice, however, is that it's almost never a good idea to offer to produce free work as a way to get your foot in the door.

No matter where you hope to work or for whom you hope to work, remember that reliability, hard work, initiative, and competence can be just as important as talent. Every piece in a portfolio needs to project these qualities, along with design ability or personal style. Very few top designers make their mark within the confines of a nine-to-five schedule. Employees who are willing to put in extra hours, solve problems, take advantage of freelance opportunities, or tackle extra projects are almost always valued. A designer who shows ambition is extremely attractive to most clients and prospective employers.

tone

The tone of a portfolio should reflect the kind of work that most interests you. If your goal is to design corporate work for a health organization, an investment firm, or a country club, it is probably appropriate for your portfolio to be elegant and formal. For this sort of client base, you should present your art in a uniform fashion, using simple gray or black mats with beveled edges or similar professional touches. This probably isn't the time to include a developmental sketchbook; rather, it is the perfect opportunity to present a box or case that's sleek and elegant. Many design schools encourage students to use foam core boards trimmed to hold their work snugly in place, or to lay ribbons under the work, allowing the viewer to pull the pieces out without damaging the foam core. This system helps to unify design projects with many different dimensions and serves to make the box more cohesive. This style of presentation appeals to many, but not all, art directors. It will likely appeal more to nondesigners, such as corporate executives, hotel or restaurant managers, or merchants who look to designers for organization and sleek packaging.

When the goal is to get work designing for younger or noncorporate audiences—perhaps CD jewel cases for a hip-hop label, book jackets, or zines—a sketchbook, along with an informal or daring presentation, is a good idea. The portfolio can be eclectic and informal, using unexpected materials and colors. Instead of aiming for a uniform look with matching mats or beveled edges, you can change the mat colors as well as the dimensions of the pieces; your case can be a purchased metal case, a handmade container, or even a vintage suitcase. You can take a unique approach to different pieces; for example, you might have a notebook with a collection of found objects, a smaller portfolio within the larger one,

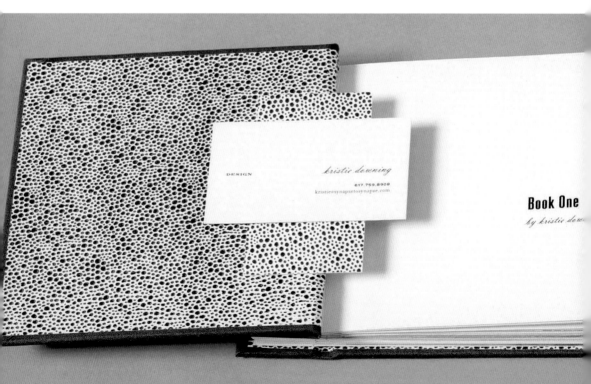

or a flipbook of photographs. Even though this portfolio might be informal, it's important that it be neat and in good order. There can never be poorly trimmed edges on boards or sloppy assembly; craftsmanship and attention to detail are important in every aspect of design.

range

Once you have determined the tone of your portfolio, be sure to show a wide range of design work. Many art directors and employers do not respond well to a portfolio unless it indicates how a designer would approach the art director or employer's area of design. For example, if a portfolio features mostly illustrated posters but no samples of text design, charts, tables, or photographs, the designer is not likely to be hired to design annual reports. There is, however, some overlap between disciplines. You don't need to have one of every item in the design lexicon. Many art directors can imagine a CD designer creating a book jacket, or a book designer creating a brochure, or an annual report designer creating a corporate identity with stationery. But it is wise for designers to produce portfolios with a wide range of design materials—more is better as long as the designer feels confident about

each piece. A good range of materials might include identity work with a letterhead and logo, a poster, product design, publication design, postage stamps, a website, and even a screensaver or a CD case. Try to include roughly twelve samples of work. Within those twelve, according to Geoffry Fried at Lesley University's Art Institute of Boston, you can group some items together, such as a set of three posters or a book series mounted together as one piece. He believes that occasional groupings of work make a great addition to a portfolio. Many schools will guide students to produce a wide variety of finished pieces as class projects for this exact reason. That being said, it's important not to pad your portfolio with repetitive, unfinished, or redundant designs.

Kristie Downing, a designer at VSA Partners in Chicago, has a relatively small 6" × 7" (15.25 × 18 cm) portfolio that has garnered praise for its simple, well-designed pages. On each spread, the left page describes the process, while the right page features an image of the finished design. The portfolio's tone is very professional, making it a good choice to show to corporations and agencies.

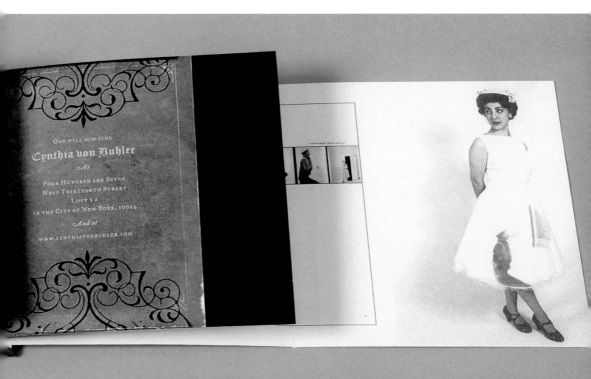

portfolios in book format

Instead of preparing traditional loose-leaf portfolios, many designers now produce bound single-edition books, attempting to unify a body of design work and experience into a cohesive whole. They arrange materials thematically or link them in a biographical manner, explaining different class projects, typographic exercises, goals, and aspirations somewhat like chapters in a book. While the traditional design portfolio sends the message that a designer is a work-horse ready to take on the next assignment, the book approach can seem extremely impressive and sophisticated. The designer presents himself or herself as a master of his or her own work and creations. In other words, book presentations tend to make designers seem more like artists and less like standard problem solvers looking to join a design staff.

Margaret Morton, a professor at Cooper Union in New York City, teaches a very demanding course titled Art of the Book. Students who take the class are committed to making personal books when they enroll. By the time they complete the course, they have gained experience in both traditional and experimental book design and binding methods. Many of these students participate in a junior-year foreign exchange program that requires them to submit a portfolio as part of the application. Morton encourages them to send a book instead of slides, as slides aren't always the best medium to show graphic design, especially if they aren't projected. She points out that the book format is practical and keeps the portfolio fluid; with the availability of personal computers and high-end printers, making a limited-edition book portfolio is now feasible where it

might not have been twenty years ago. Morton says her design mentors always stressed the idea of analyzing design shifts and trends within the broader context of technological advancements.

Morton's students aren't the only young designers creating books. Louise Sandhaus at California Institute of the Arts (CalArts), in Valencia, California, requires her graduate students to make a book that both documents and reflects their studies. Although these are specific class projects and are not intended as portfolios, they often become substitutes for portfolios because they can be produced in multiple editions, mailed, and even left with the recipient. Geoffry Fried of the Art Institute of Boston points out that a well-done book of this type can be a home run, because it is so well written, designed, and produced that it takes the place of the more traditional grouping of school assignments. Noted designer Ellen

Lupton and her students at the Maryland Institute College of Art have also put together a book about design for publication. Lupton's students used their design samples as content and collaborated with her on the text. This project makes both a unique presentation within a portfolio and an impressive give-away portfolio when necessary.

There are some drawbacks, however. Book portfolios, like websites, show your work as a group of reproductions, and as such they're a step away from the original design. The viewer cannot see the original size or experience the tactile qualities of the original materials, including three-dimensional features such as foldouts, pop-ups, or variations in paper stock. Many art directors even feel a sentimental attraction to slightly unpolished art school design projects, which can be particularly attractive in the sterile one-dimensional world of computers.

Brian Roettinger produced *Lost and Found* in preparation for his graduation from the California Institute of the Arts.

ABOVE and OPPOSITE
Lost and Found includes photos of his posters
held by fellow students or being mounted on walls.
Because the posters are shown in relation to people, the
viewer is able to estimate the scale and weight of each
piece. This type of book is easy to produce and send to
art directors without the worry of loss that comes with
traditional portfolios.

ABOVE
This page of Roettinger's book explains various pieces
in the portfolio. The text offers a visual pause and gives
the viewer a context for reviewing the posters.

showing process

Many design directors like to see thumbnails, rough sketches, or text pages that reveal the path taken to the final design solution. Thumbnails are a good way to gain insight into a designer's methodology; the images allow a designer to explain the problem that was presented, restrictions that were imposed, or any specifications from the teacher or client. A creative director with design training is likely to respond favorably to thumbnails and developmental sketches.

That being said, explanations and thumbnails are more appropriate for some interviews than others. A restaurant owner hiring a design firm to design menus, signs, and a logo may be less interested in the thought process behind the problem than the solution itself. The restaurant owner is probably more interested in seeing samples of successful design work created for popular and profitable restaurants. A creative director, on the other hand, wants to know how a designer thinks and arrives at solutions. One way to offer something for both types of clients is to use foldouts or flaps that reveal developmental sketches.

This way the viewer can opt to investigate thumbnails and descriptive copy or ignore them.

Another approach, used successfully by the design firm Modern Dog in Seattle, is to include some developmental variations and alternatives for a few select pieces at the beginning of the portfolio. Modern Dog includes a limited-edition matchbook style book of logos with a flowered paper cover as part of a larger group of design products. The piece opens with several introductory paragraphs that discuss the complexity of professional logo design in a world where everyone wants to be a designer. Next come two samples of logos, showing developmental work and explanatory text along with the finished logos. These examples are extremely helpful in understanding the firm's design ethos and problem-solving methodology. Finally, the reader encounters a series of finished logos covering a wide array of subjects, from soap and software to the state lottery.

This little logo book by Modern Dog is a perfect example of showing process in a portfolio. The text on the right facing page, shown below, describes the problem as it was presented to the design firm, and the images on the left show several variations that preceded the final design.

Case Study: Mercer & Company
Seattle, Washington

Logo for a womenswear retail store. The Mercer business model: bring contemporary fashion — mostly jeans and t-shirts — to women aged 25-50 who are on the go, and give them a shopping alternative that is both convenient and fun.

Owner Scott Bonomo told us, that if Mercer was a car, it would be a restored 356 Porsche Speedster. He also told us he likened the Mercer image to an old New York City warehouse district sign. So that's where we started. The comps on the left were pulled from the first round.

create flexible content

A third and highly effective method for presenting both work and process is to tuck a separate sketchbook into the back of your presentation box or portfolio, which you can remove and show upon request. Portfolios are best when you can adjust and rearrange content. The ability to add or delete pieces is crucial to making your book appropriate for any particular interview. Having a separate process book offers the best of both worlds; it's available if you need it and hidden if you don't.

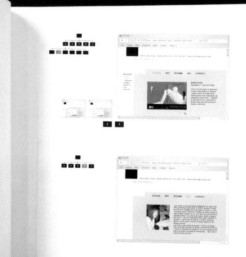

Several pages from a classic student process book, developed by Melissa Merlet of Simmons College in Boston during her senior year, reveal a great deal about how a young designer arrives at a design solution. Developmental sketches can be highly informative to an art director and can spark a discussion between employer and potential employee about the thought process.

Robin Lynch, a design professor at the State University of New York at Purchase, believes that designers should always show process in their portfolios, regardless of the potential employer's design training. She advises her students to carry a sketch or process book with them at all times so they can enlighten and engage prospective employers by showing the thought process that led to a good design solution. Melle Hammer, cofounder of the working symposium DesignInquiry in Portland, Maine, agrees. He thinks that looking at a design piece without some understanding of how formal decisions were made is meaningless during a review of a designer's work.

Ultimately, it is essential to keep a presentation flexible during an interview. It is up to you to subtly control an interview whenever possible, adjusting the order and depth of the presentation intuitively to match the interest of the client or art director. You must remain aware of what a prospective employer is looking for and rearrange the content on the spot if necessary. If a client is responding well to sketches, continue to show them. When the viewer begins to look bored, move on.

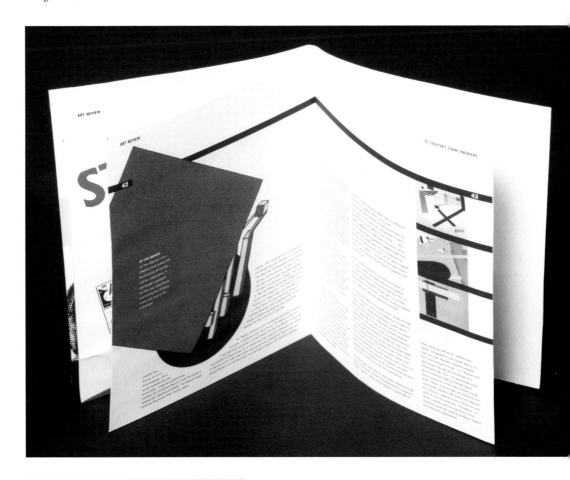

To further the understanding, final printed products can be shown in relationship to the process book to help illustrate how the ideas featured developed into finished solutions.

Presentation Boxes, Cases, and Portfolios

choosing the proper package

Making a live portfolio presentation is still one of the best ways for a designer to get a new job or secure freelance work. Each company and potential employer is unique, so you must tailor your presentation to fit the situation, be prepared to answer questions about your design process, and familiarize yourself with a potential client's history and recent work.

It's often said that the larger the dimensions of the portfolio, the less experienced the applicant. Oversized samples are the domain of students with big vision and strong backs. As a designer matures, his or her work often becomes more compact and portable. There are definite advantages to having a portfolio that fits neatly in a Federal Express box.

1

2

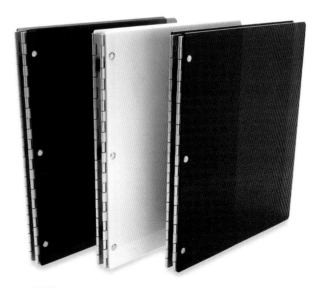

3

1, 2 Bookcase portfolios are versatile in form and function and offer a tailored presentation. The clamshell design acts as both a portfolio book and a presentation case. It has an acrylic 3" × 5" (7.6 × 12.7 cm) window for added personalization, as well as a steel multiring mechanism, retractable black vinyl handle, and Velcro closures.

3 The aluminum screw post in this portfolio is designed to lie perfectly flat when opened. This type of portfolio is available in several dimensions. All are made of satin-finish aluminum with sheet protectors, mounting sheets, hinge strips, protective jackets, and screw post extensions. Nylon jackets are also available to protect the portfolio from light, dust, and scratches.

4 This sleek portfolio features screw post covers that are made of $^1/_8$" (3 mm) durable acrylic, come in classic colors, and are available in three standard formats. You can also purchase nylon jackets to protect your books.

4

No matter what size your work, you have a wealth of options for presenting it. A wide variety of companies produce manufactured portfolios, as well as customized, one-of-a-kind portfolios and presentation boxes. Different kinds of portfolios work best for different types of clients, and everyone responds to various formats in his or her own way.

More important than the type of box, however, is the condition of the materials inside. When choosing a portfolio case or box, make sure everything fits snugly so your samples can't slide around and become damaged or get out of order. Clients and employers expect graphic designers to be neat and organized, so your samples should look clean and newly printed. If everything fits snugly in your portfolio, your samples should remain in pristine condition. (You also want them to stay neat because you may have only one or two copies of each.)

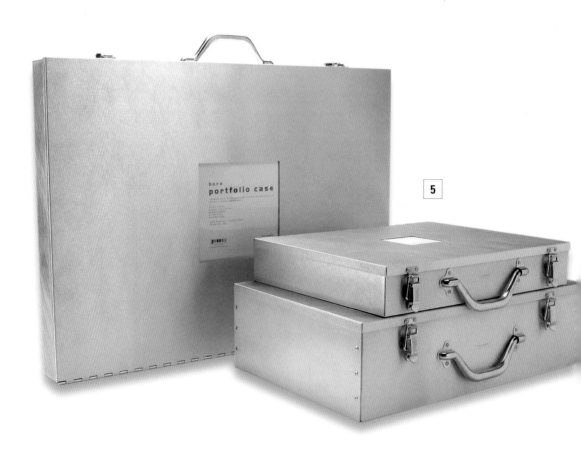

boro
portfolio case

5

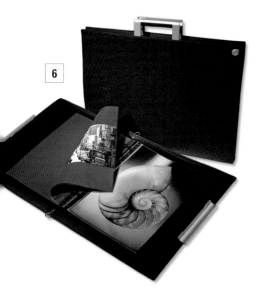

6

5 These aluminum presentation cases come in three sizes (12" × 15" × 2.5", 12" × 18" × 5", and 18" × 25" × 2.5" [30.5 × 63.5 × 6.4 cm, 30.5 × 45.7 × 12.7 cm, and 45.7 × 63.5 × 6.4 cm]) so you can pick the one that best accommodates your work.

6 Made of dark canvas or linen, this stylish professional presentation case is stiff enough to hold your work in place but also light enough not to add unnecessary weight. The retractable handles are made of brushed chrome, and the portfolio has a good-quality zipper with an interior ring binder that holds extra archival-quality polypropylene sleeves. The work stays pristine, and you can replace old work with new whenever necessary.

7 This sleek portfolio book features vinyl sleeves, which protects your work and allow you to replace old work with new whenever necessary. With an exterior of smooth imitation black leather, it's a popular choice that's readily available in many art stores.

8 This high-end portfolio book comes in genuine black leather tanned in Italy and features removable pages. For designers who want to appear corporate and sophisticated, this portfolio has great appeal.

7

8

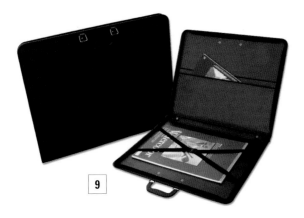

9

9 Traditional portfolios in black simulated leather are sold in many art stores around the world and are also available through online art stores.

10 Made for CDs, this double jewel case, made of scratch-resistant, anodized aluminum, holds two CDs stacked one above the other and provides a display pocket that accommodates 4.75" (12.1 cm) square sheets. This alternative is perfect for those looking for a traditional yet sophisticated package for a digital presentation.

11 Expandable and simple, package portfolios feature standard screw post configurations, so they are compatible with all major brands of sheet protectors, mounting sheets, and adhesive hinge strips. This simple design allows the pages to lie flat and offers a slim profile that can be expanded by means of extensions. A nylon jacket is also available to protect the portfolio from light, dust, and scratches.

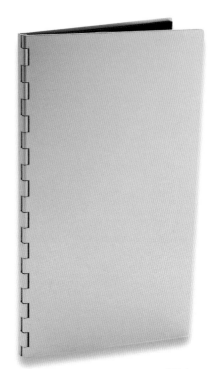

10

district screwpost portfolio book

11

PRESENTATION BOXES come in many formats, and the selection is constantly changing. Leather, imitation leather, book cloth, and lightweight metal are the most common exterior materials. The boxes frequently have handles or shoulder straps for easy carrying. If you search on the Internet or shop in metropolitan art stores, you might also find clamshells and boxes made from a wide variety of materials. Although black imitation leather is very common, you may be able to find stainless steel boxes. Some designers like to use photographers' presentation boxes, which are made of sturdy aluminum, with felt or foam lining inside.

If you want something more original, look through the photo album sections in art, gift, or stationery stores. These albums are often well made and come in a wider selection of colors. Because they may not have handles, however, you'll need to think creatively about how to carry the portfolio. Sometimes sports and luggage stores have simple well-designed cloth cases that can fit snugly around a box or album without handles. Or you could fit an album inside a traditional presentation box, or a box within a box. A good way to break your portfolios into segments is to put one category of work into a small box or ring binder, with loose samples in the larger box. Finally, there are all kinds of unusual options—from vintage suitcases (page 154) to old record boxes (page 164). These can be dynamic options for the right kind of design portfolio.

The most important ideas for presentation boxes boil down to the obvious. A great portfolio needs to be light enough so it can be easily carried over ten city blocks on the way to an interview or appointment. In addition, it needs to hold up—over multiple interviews—without becoming damaged. These are simple points, but if you overlook them, they can cost you a lot of time and unnecessary expense.

12

12 A simple, elegant solution, these well-made boxes (left) are covered in book cloth and allow you to assemble items of several different sizes without commissioning a custom box. They come in ten colors and have a shallow depth of 2.25" (5.7 cm). Also covered in book cloth (and available in ten colors), this box (right) has a deeper capacity, 5.5" × 7.75" × 9.25" (13.4 × 19.7 × 23.5 cm), which leaves room for more samples.

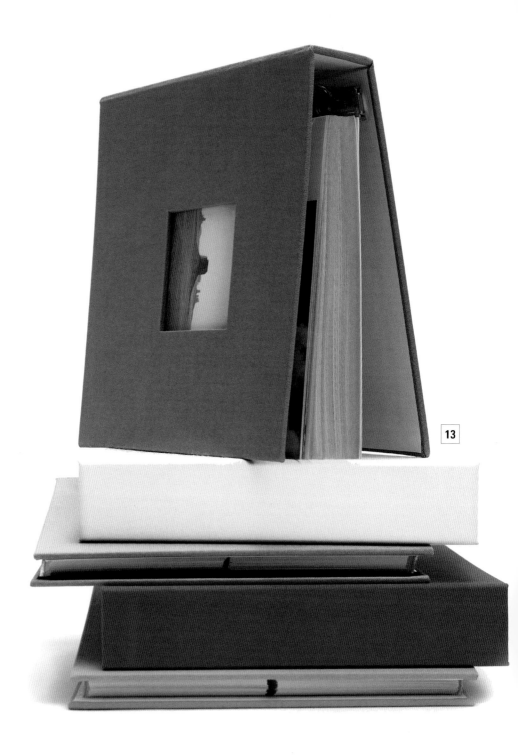

13

13 These multicolored photo albums contain ring binders that hold half-page polypropylene sleeves. The boards are made of double-thick, fully archival material to avoid warping. With an exterior covered in European book cloth and a choice of ten colors, this kind of album is a stylish choice. The albums are 8.25" × 7.25" (21 × 18.4 cm) and have a small square window where you can insert a personal image or business card.

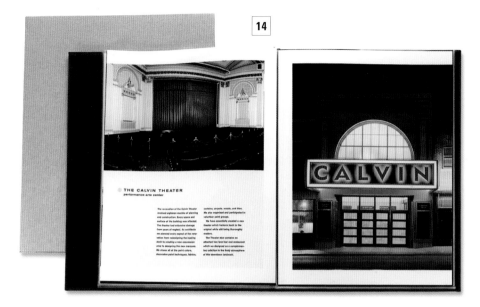

14 These albums, covered in book cloth, feature full-page polypropylene sleeves. With an overall size of 9.25" × 12.25" (23.5 × 31 cm), they can easily double as portfolios. The top-loading protector pages hold 8.5" × 11" (21.6 × 27.9 cm) samples.

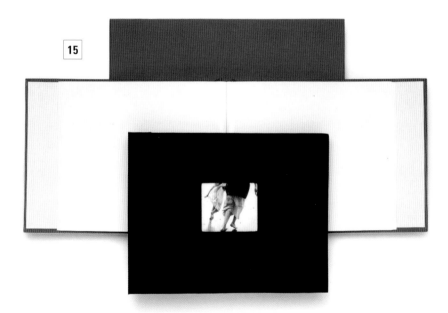

15 Bound in European book cloth, this album is really designed to be a scrapbook. It has double-thick archival boards, and you can add or remove pages. You can also run the pages through an ink-jet printer. The album comes in three dimensions: 8.5" × 11" (21.6 × 27.9 cm), 11" × 14" (27.9 × 35.6 cm), and 12" × 13.5" (30.5 × 34.3 cm). It also has a window for inserting a business card or picture and is available in ten colors.

Advice from Professionals

When it comes to portfolio format, Chris Pullman, vice president of WGBH television in Boston and design professor at Yale University, prefers a simple box of "whatever proportion suits the need." The presentation case or box should allow the contents to be free-floating rather than stuffed into the scratched sleeves of a ring binder with pages that get stuck. Worse yet are designs trapped inside hardened plastic casings with felt backs that look like a set of cheap placemats. Pullman says a box doesn't need to be fancy or have fussy compartments; it just needs to be full of well-designed pieces that are in perfect shape and accompanied by captions or thumbnails to inform the viewer about the design process.

Be sure to get as many samples as possible, so you can refresh your portfolio when the art gets damaged. It is important to find a system for making sure artwork is packed tightly, perhaps by adding a simple piece of foam to keep things from sliding, scratching, and crumpling at the edges. If you choose foam core for mounting, it should be clean and free of dents. Mats can also be effective. You should always include a well-designed résumé, along with business cards and a giveaway CD loaded with PDFs showing your work. Although a digital presentation is not always the best way to see the work initially, a leave-behind CD can be a great reminder for those who have reviewed

your portfolio in the flesh. All three of these elements should feature the same typeface and color system, creating an identity for you.

Sometimes, the most memorable portfolios are those that aren't over designed or complicated to reassemble. As director of the design department at WGBH and a teacher at the Rhode Island School of Design, Doug Scott has seen thousands of portfolios pass through his office. His favorite was a presentation box with a ring-binder portfolio that filled precisely half the box and contained mounted, flat pieces. The rest of the material—various brochures, booklets, and larger pieces—fit perfectly into the remaining half of the box. The portfolio had a faultless combination of materials and a case in which everything fit simply and securely.

Elizabeth Resnick, chair of the design department at the Massachusetts College of Art in Boston, helps her students master presentation skills by making sure they get plenty of practice. She requires young designers to start thinking about portfolios as early as their sophomore year. By senior year, they've completed a course in portfolio development and are comfortable with the idea of presenting samples in person. Resnick's students generally favor presentation boxes over ring binders. If they're energetic and willing, students are encouraged by the portfolio professor to make their own cloth-covered books filled with foam core for mounting samples and artwork. The result is lovely, durable, economical, and unique.

At Simmons College, there is a different philosophy when it comes to preparing for graduation. Students take courses that focus on design samples for their portfolio rather than the portfolio itself. Judith Aronson, graphic design professor, discontinued the portfolio class three years ago in favor of courses that help students put together polished assignments worthy of a portfolio. Since there are no hard-and-fast rules about what graduating students must include in a portfolio, these presentations might include everything from Web and motion work to photography, corporate identity work to brochures, or various types of publications. The range of boxes and cases is as broad as the work, though most students choose small presentation boxes that are no larger than a briefcase. Aronson stresses that the box is secondary to the work and should never be too distracting.

Hyan Auh's résumé, card, and miniaccordion portfolio are carefully designed in proportion and use the same typeface, logo, and overall look, creating a unified presentation. The front and back covers of the miniportfolio are Auh's business cards. One is attached to the front, and the other can be removed by the client or prospective employer.

By sandwiching two mats together and cutting a window into the top one, an inset is created, which neatly displays a CD. A simple ribbon fastened within the inset makes it easy to remove the CD without damaging the mats.

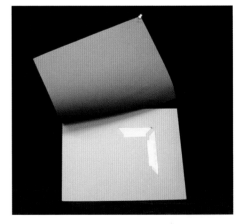

The front and back of a mounted sleeve can hold artwork in place on a mat. Acetate triangles fit through slits in the board, making a tight folder. These cards were designed as a keepsake for an AIGA exhibition of Paul Rand's work displayed at the Massachusetts College of Art in Boston.

BOARDS for mounting artwork come in two materials: mat board, which is a durable, high-quality cardboard, and foam core, which is a Styrofoam product with a protective semigloss coating on either side. Both are available at most art stores.

MAT BOARD comes in a variety of weights, dimensions, and colors, and some feature different colors on the front and back. The most elegant type however, is museum board. Acid-free and archival, it can be beveled more successfully than typical mats. Museum board is most commonly white, off-white, black, or gray, but you can find other colors at frame shops and larger art stores. A bevel is usually used when a mat is cut to exhibit a mounted piece, such as an 8" × 10" (20.3 × 25.4 cm) transparency or an unfinished work with rough edges that must be hidden. When choosing mat board however, a critical factor is weight. Although durability is important, take into consideration the combined weight of all the boards and choose materials that make sense for your situation. You want to be sure that the end result is easy to carry and affordable to send.

FOAM CORE is another common choice for an alternative mounting material. It comes in many colors, several widths, and has the advantage of being lighter than most mats. But while foam core is lightweight, it's also bulky. Typically, half as many foam core boards will fit into your case as mats. Another slight disadvantage is that foam core will disintegrate a bit around the edges with time.

Be aware, however, that both mat board and foam core can fold and wrinkle, eventually suffering crushed corners and dinged edges. Also, be aware that learning to successfully cut each of these products takes time and skill. If you haven't done it before, buy a few extra sheets for practice.

At the Rhode Island School of Design in Providence, most students are encouraged to use museum board or mat board to mount design pieces, but their teachers also advise them to leave some pieces unmounted. The opinion of many design directors is that mounted work can seem altered and overly formal. Good design can and should stand on its own in an honest, unadorned manner. Depending on the type of work they hope to get, designers may create an entirely informal portfolio without any mounted pieces. If you choose to mount your sample work, according to graduating RISD designer Lauren Criscione, you can use a variety of methods to secure the pieces to the board: spray adhesive (used outdoors while wearing a face mask), glue stick, double-sided tape, or a dry adhesive such as StudioTac (little white dots with glue on the back, sold in sheets).

Advice from the Professionals

Art pieces such as CD packages can be placed inside hand-made acetate sleeves, which are then mounted onto mat board. Judith Aronson, from Simmons College, instructs her students to make these sleeves from triangular acetate shapes. Cut heavyweight acetate into a triangle slightly larger than is needed to hold the CD. The extra length will become two hidden flaps. Make two perpendicular slits in the center of the board. Crease the extra edges of acetate and slip them through to the back side of the mat board, then tape them in place. Affix a second board to the back of this presentation to hide the tape on the back of the first piece.

The best product Aronson advises her students to use when making all kinds of presentations and binding materials for class or portfolio pieces is Micropore tape, a Johnson & Johnson product, found in the first-aid section of any pharmacy. It is flexible, reusable, and incredibly strong for making bindings and gatefolds on mounted pieces or books.

RING BINDERS come in many sizes, colors, and materials. They can be classic black imitation leather cases with zippers down the side, which range roughly from 12" × 8" (30.5 × 20.3 cm) to 4' × 3' (122.9 × 91.4 cm). Alternatively, you can find simple and relatively small ring binders that are sometimes used as photo albums. Most ring binders have vinyl sleeves for artwork. These sleeves allow you to slip in new samples, adding and subtracting artwork according to need. The outer edge of the classic ring binder portfolio usually has a zipper to protect the contents from damage.

Ring binders, however, aren't without drawbacks. The sleeves can become scratched with time, and the artwork occasionally slips out of position and you have to realign it while politely apologizing to the client or prospective employer. In addition, the plastic sleeves sometimes get stuck in the rings of the binder, which creates the need for more polite apologies during a presentation.

But Janet Odgis, principal of Odgis + Company in Manhattan, prefers classic sleeves in a ring binder to presentation boxes. Because she does mostly corporate identity work, Odgis wants clients to be able to pull brochures, booklets, and product work out of the portfolio for closer examination. She likes the client to be able to hold and experience the actual printed objects; to her, it feels more honest than a mounted presentation. Sleeves also offer surprising versatility. Odgis has included items as diverse as a folded canvas bag in her portfolio. She keeps extra sleeves on hand to replace any that become scratched or smoky. She also makes her binder presentation unique by keeping it in a custom-made cloth-covered box.

1

2

1 Classic and simple: This binder features a durable, woven, and nylon-backed black PVC cover that will withstand wear and tear. Multiring portfolio books allow you to tailor your portfolio quickly and easily for a particular client or interview.

2 Alternative color: This three-ring binder is also available in black and silver. It offers an alternative color for those seeking an unusual presentation.

3 These satin-finish aluminum portfolios feature flat spines and steel multiring hardware. They come in two sizes, 8.5" × 11" (21.6 × 27.9 cm) and 11" × 14" (27.9 × 35.6 cm), and have ten polyester sheet protectors and a black nylon presentation jacket.

4 This soft exterior case made of a canvaslike fabric is great for transporting groups of stiff presentation boards with maximum care. Because of the lightweight fabric, the overall weight of the portfolio is greatly reduced, making it easier to carry to interviews.

3

4

INEXPENSIVE PRESENTATION MATERIALS

Sometimes, a designer may choose or need to create a great presentation from less expensive stationery store materials. This might occur when a designer doesn't have time to pull together a formal portfolio. For example, a staff designer might get a call out of the blue from a competitor looking to fill a position. With a portfolio that has not been updated for five years, the designer has to create something new and fresh for a meeting and presentation the following day.

A simple and inexpensive portfolio might also be a good match for certain design work. When Kobi Benezri at *I.D.* magazine sent me his portfolio, it included eight to ten magazines, one book, and a school portfolio—all placed in an economical and disposable cardboard magazine box. It was a perfect presentation choice for an eclectic group of items, especially since the box had a logical connection to his main body of work at *I.D.* magazine.

In a similar vein, Min Wang, design professor at China Central Academy of Fine Arts, sent a selection of materials—a book, a promotional brochure, a cover letter, and a résumé—gathered into a transparent plastic folder. He had chosen this inexpensive folder to fit the exact dimensions of his portfolio materials. Although the folder was economical, it was the perfect solution. Designers can and should make use of practical materials even when they're common and inexpensive. Part of a designer's skill is to be the curator of all things well designed, regardless of cost.

Kobi Benezri, art director of *I.D.* magazine, assembled his portfolio, shown below, in a simple cardboard magazine box. There is a point in a designer's career when a simple idea such as this one can be just right. In this case, most of Benezri's portfolio consists of issues of *I.D.*

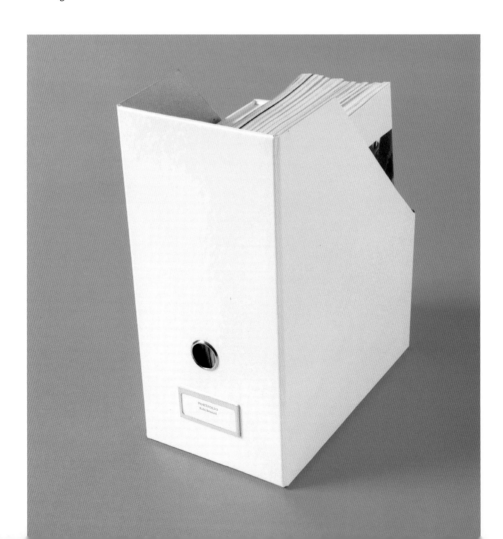

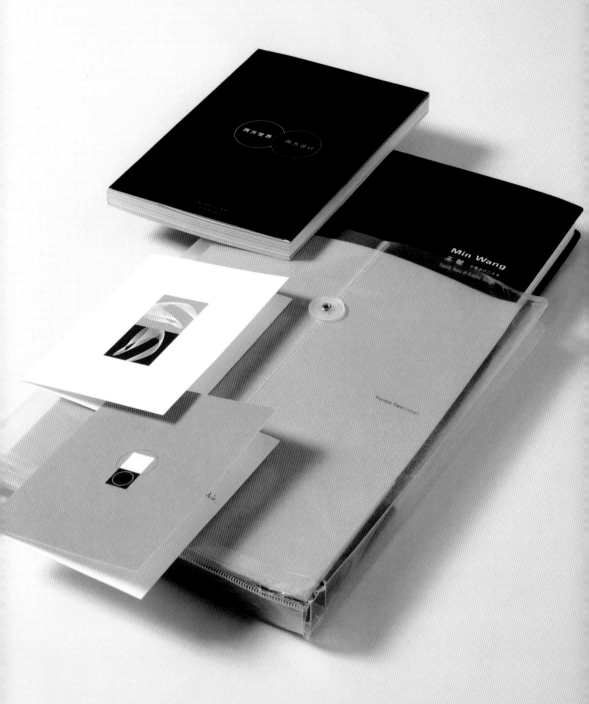

In this picture, you can see Min Wang's simple transparent plastic envelope. The cards hold all four pieces in place and unify the presentation simply and efficiently.

Presenting a Print Portfolio

the order of things

A critical part of any presentation is the order of elements. The first thing in your portfolio or presentation box should be a strong design sample—a drum roll to get the viewer excited or, at the very least, engaged. It should probably not be your very best piece, but it needs to catch attention and hold it. The dimension and structure of the binder or box will play a role in determining how you organize things. Beyond that, you should position your pieces in an order that will build anticipation and excitement until, at last, you show the highlight of your work. When making a live presentation, you're the master of ceremonies: you can adjust the order of work as you go, pulling things out from behind and placing them in a new order, lingering on specific works, or moving rapidly over certain portions. It's important to pay attention to the client's reactions, moving on when they look disinterested, or talking in depth about a piece that seems to pique his or her interest. These skills will serve you well throughout your career. Think of your portfolio presentation as a piece of music; you're the conductor, setting the tempo and rhythm.

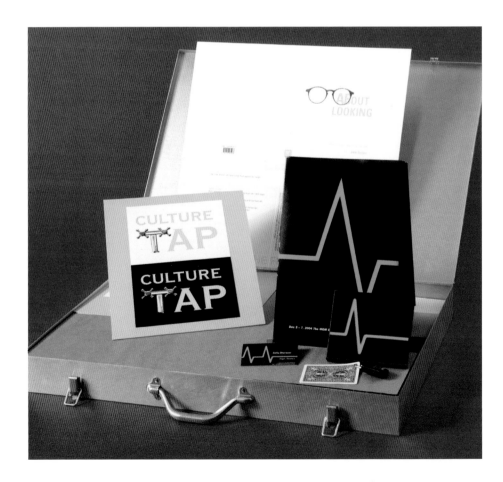

A large portion of MassArt graduate Crista Hirzel's work deals with social responsibility and environmental issues. The theme of ecology is consistent throughout her portfolio, and she has emphasized that theme by choosing simple cardboard as her packing material.

This portfolio from Simmons College communication design student Sarah Curran is attractive and practical; the red lightweight cardboard is easy to open, unfolding like an envelope.

Inside Curran's portfolio, she mounts class projects and covers them with simple brown kraft paper to protect them from damage.

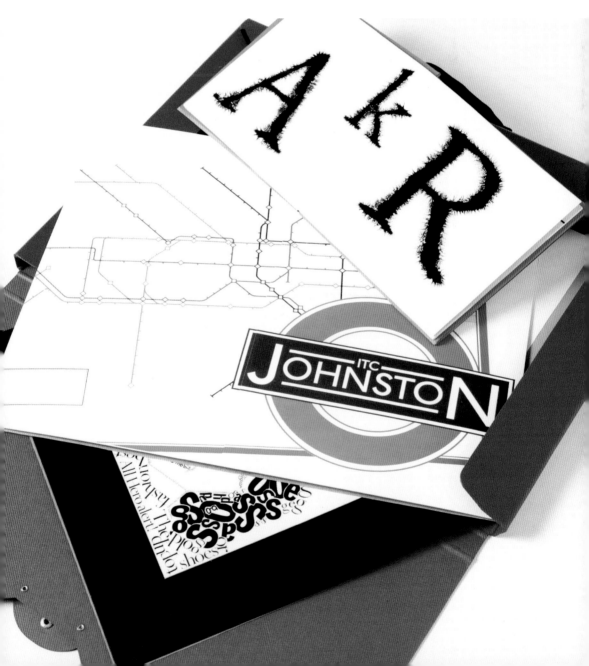

In addition, you need to give some thought to the cohesiveness of your entire body of work. It should be, according to Geoffry Fried, "an ensemble with a purpose." Even if you are assembling four years' worth of class projects into a single portfolio, it's still important to rework or polish old pieces and to unify them in a thematic way. Careful thought as to order and consistency of components can only make the presentation better. The choices you make in forming your portfolio are of interest, so if you are passionate about art history or ecology, you can and should work these themes in. Remember that a good portfolio should express in some subtle way who you are and what relationship you have to the world. This will separate you from other designers and help the interviewer understand more about you.

If you cannot be present for a portfolio presentation, it is important to have a portfolio that is easy to reassemble. Having too many complex insets that look like puzzle pieces quickly becomes aggravating for a busy art director. The system for taking things out of the box or case and putting them back should be simple and intuitive. In addition, be sure to include some text or captions to help explain the work in your absence.

preparing

The most effective way to land work is through in-person presentations or interviews, but it's crucial to plan ahead. It's a good idea to make a list of potential interview questions and practice answering them beforehand. Remember that an interview is more about having a conversation with the potential employer than a show-and-tell. The interviewer wants to get to know more about you, what interests you most about design, and how you formulate ideas or make choices. To go one step further, set up a mock presentation with a friend posing as the interviewer. Ask him or her to be critical of some of your work, so you can rehearse fielding negative feedback. This exercise gives you the chance to practice defending your choices—an ability that art directors and creative

directors like to see. An experienced designer can talk intelligently about what he or she has done and why, so be prepared to discuss a design solution at length but leave out frustrations or negative anecdotes whenever possible.

presenting

First impressions can make or break an interview or presentation, so it is extremely important to be on time. Don't arrive half an hour early and expect the interviewer to usher you in; five minutes early is good, but more than ten can be irritating. If you have to be late, call beforehand and explain, but if it's a casual excuse such as "I overslept," you've probably already lost the job. Be courteous and maintain a professional demeanor, which includes remembering the name of the company and interviewer, and do your best to be articulate about your work.

Make it a point to keep the tone of all your comments positive. Never speak apologetically or dismissively about anything you've done. If you aren't confident about a particular design piece, you shouldn't be featuring it in your portfolio. Since designers must present or sell their solutions to clients everyday, good presentation skills are a critical part of a designer's skill set. The interviewer will be looking closely at your ability to present or sell your own work.

New graduates sometimes make the mistake of referring to their class experience too specifically in early interviews. Rather than saying, "This poster is a typography exercise from Type 101," it is better to point out that you enjoyed making the poster because, for example, you became more

In advance of finished work, designer Deborah Norcross' portfolio shows page after page of work in progress. Ideas are shown worked, reworked, flipped upside down, inverted, rotated, and in various color combinations, sizes, and shapes preceding the finished product. Her portfolio is like an invitation backstage to see the ideas and process behind the finished product.

knowledgeable about the specific typeface used and the history of typography. School should not be the main context with which you present and describe the pieces in your portfolio.

When you present your portfolio, you're showing the work you've already created. But the second and more important part of the equation is letting the interviewer know what kind of work you'll be able to produce if you're awarded the job or position. You should not list goals, verbalize a mission statement, or say something along the lines of "Here's what I can do for you," because you risk sounding arrogant. There is, however, the opportunity to exhibit competence, confidence, openness, and acuity—all traits that are positive indicators of future job performance. To do this, you'll need careful preparation, a bit of instinct, and good manners.

FORMAT PREFERENCES Of the three types of portfolios that he reviews, Chris Pullman of WGBH public television in the United States prefers print portfolios to websites or motion portfolios. First, they present fewer obstacles and difficulties. Because they don't rely on technology, many variables and frustrations associated with speed or software incompatibility are eliminated. Second, designers with print portfolios generally tend to offer a deeper level of understanding about their work. They often deconstruct and explain limitations and talk about research or time/budget issues that may have occurred.

The most important quality Pullman looks for in a portfolio presentation is the applicant's ability to speak intelligently about his or her work. "If you cannot be present when your portfolio is being reviewed, then it is imperative to provide written commentary on the work to accompany the portfolio." Explanatory text should include "the exact problem to be solved" and the process followed when creating the finished product.

This provides an interviewer with insight into your thought process and your ability to communicate in writing—a valuable skill in itself.

Pullman likes to see as much of a designer's skill set and design process as possible. Showing preliminary sketches and alternate designs shows a designer's range and capability for problem solving. He also likes to see any extra contributions a designer made to a project, including drawings, written work, diagrams, or artwork—anything from tables, charts, and maps to legends or photography. Finally, he dislikes spreads that have been mounted on foam core because he'd prefer to see the product in its original form.

The way you present yourself can be as important as your portfolio. Pullman says he forms his first impression after hearing the elevator door open and watching a prospective designer take ten steps down the hall. He does not expect an applicant to be formally dressed, but "each piece of the way a person presents themselves" makes an impact. Before you go on an interview, it's important to think carefully about every detail. For example, make sure your clothes are not stained or covered with cat hair, that you are not missing a belt loop or sporting misaligned buttons. Pullman points out that everything gives him a small clue about how carefully a person thinks about the fine points, of how much of a perfectionist he or she is.

Pullman describes his staff as a family that functions most efficiently when there is harmony between all the members. He will not hire an applicant who interrupts incessantly or acts aloof, egotistical, disorganized, or unfocused. Pullman says he used to ask applicants what they would bring to a company potluck supper just to see how quickly and creatively their minds work. As he says, "The meta presentation is almost as important as the things in the portfolio."

This page in Norcross' book shows the stages of her design for an invitation to a Grammy party.

Job Hunting

cold calls

A phone call, rather than an email, is still the proper method of contacting a potential employer or client to drum up freelance work or an interview. Creative directors have busy schedules, and tracking down designers who are away or busy can be frustrating and a waste of time. Knowing a freelance designer is free and available for new work can be just what they need, so do not hesitate to make a call to let them know. Ask an art director what time of year is best to call, and be persistent without nagging or calling too often. Also, freelance designers can and should ask whether the art director prefers to receive calls or mailers as follow-up reminders. Giving the client a choice is perfectly reasonable and often appreciated.

Before picking up the phone, be sure to do your homework first. Here are some guidelines to help you make a good first impression:

- Compile a list of art directors or companies. There are many sources to find this type of information, including:
  - Design magazines
  - Magazine mastheads
  - Company websites
  - *Literary Marketplace* (LMP), a reference book that lists the names and contact information for art directors at publishing houses throughout the United States, and the *International Literary Marketplace*, which lists publishers outside of the United States.
  - Design organizations can be found on the International Council of Graphic Design Association's website, www.icograda.org. Icograda is the professional world body for graphic design and visual communication.
  - Faculty lists from design school websites
  - Advertising annuals (Clio, Art Directors Club, Hatch, Summit Creative Awards), ADDY (American Advertising Federation), and BTAA (British Television Advertising Award)
  - Grammy Awards and the various video music awards will provide contacts in the music industry.
- Find out the name of the person with whom you should be speaking and ask for them specifically. Knowing the correct person to speak with shows your attention to detail and illustrates your level of interest in the job.
- Mentioning an art director's recent projects or awards can be flattering and will illustrate your level of interest in the job.
- Use a reliable landline phone, rather than a cell phone or cordless phone, if possible.
- Present your name first before addressing the person you are contacting.
- Keep the conversation polite, brief, and on track.
- Do not answer call waiting, and never put the art director or creative director on hold.
- Ask if the art director sees portfolios and try to set up an appointment where you can present your work in person. If this is not possible, but they have a drop-off day when you can leave your portfolio for viewing, this is your next best option. Drop-offs are not ideal because there is no way to ensure the art director will review your work or for you to gauge his or her reaction to it.
- Many art directors prefer to see design samples in advance of a portfolio, so be prepared to provide the following: PDFs by email, a URL of a website where your work is posted, or print samples by regular mail.
- If an art director does not want to see you or your samples, ask if there is a better time in the year to call back, and bring the conversation to an amicable close. It is reasonable to try back a year later, so use a file or notebook during a job search to keep track of who you spoke with, when you spoke, any important details in the conversation, and his or her contact information.

résumés

Résumés are the perfect chance to illustrate one's ability to compose elegant and legible type on a beautiful sheet of paper. A good résumé is critical, both in terms of design and content, and many art directors will not see someone if his or her résumé is poorly designed. Similarly, some principals have hired designers based on a résumé alone. Many designers fail to make the most of the opportunity to design their résumés as well as they design their primary work. By investing all their energy in an overdesigned personal logo or decorative element rather than the structure of the document, they miss the chance to produce strong information design that reflects their talents. Here are some suggestions that will help ensure your résumé is legible, easy to follow, and well designed.

- As in a table of contents, your résumé must offer several levels of information within a consistent and clear hierarchy.
- Use nonaligning figures rather than standard numerals for a more elegant presentation.
- Use properly spaced small caps or traditional upper- and lowercase letters for headings instead of all caps.
- Avoid type that is too small or too pale, and make sure it's big enough to be read easily.
- Whether serif or sans serif, new or classic, the type should be highly legible.
- Avoid the latest trendy typeface in favor of a font you know well and would normally use for text design.
- Do not follow a standardized résumé format at the expense of good typography—your résumé should look as though a designer created it.
- Type should be kerned well, and if type is unjustified, create an elegant rag or vertical edge.
- Your email address and phone number should not be smaller than 10- or 11-point type, depending on the face.

These two résumés at right were produced by Alissa Miller. She created the first version (top) before consulting with Judith Aronson, and the second (bottom) afterward. For her first résumé, Miller followed standard résumé formatting with centered caps for headings and flush-left type for the entries; it is serviceable but not of the caliber of design that art directors expect. By contrast, her new résumé is sophisticated and well designed, using legible, contemporary type in readable flush-left columns. In addition, her text has improved significantly and the dates have been simplified.

- Choose a color for the text that is dark enough to read easily—black is best. Type that is very light can cause eyestrain for the reader.
- Choose colors wisely. Résumés with yellow or pale gray can appear to lack confidence.
- Use high-quality printer paper in a color and dimension that reflects your business card, portfolio color, and overall design system.
- Your choice in paper stock must not interfere with legibility in any way, so be careful of papers that are too dark or highly textured.
- Follow the rules of grammar and punctuation—always.
- Pay careful attention to hyphenation. Don't hyphenate proper nouns if you can help it; hyphenate at logical places, and try not to have three end-of-line hyphens in a stack.
- Ask as many people as you can, including a friend or a colleague with good writing skills, to edit your résumé.
- Always use spell check, but do not rely on it. Have your documents proofread several times.
- Give thought to how your résumé will fold into an envelope and whether the fold will—or should—affect the design.

Hyun Auh, a recent graduate from the FIT (Fashion Institute of Technology), designed a résumé that slips perfectly inside his portfolio just like any other page, forming a clean presentation. His portfolio has a fold-in that creates a flap or cover, shown at right below. One important aspect of the package is Auh's attention to detail. His portfolio, résumé, and business card maintain the same proportion to scale and are precisely coordinated for a tight presentation.

The information you include on your résumé is, of course, just as important as its design. Remember to include the following:
- A basic list of relevant internships and jobs (preferably in reverse chronological order), as well as educational background and degrees, seminars and conferences attended, and any awards and honors received.
- Any design- and art-related skills, such as photography, filmmaking, drawing, illustration, production work, or printmaking. Because many design firms now have copy writing and marketing departments, any training or competency in these areas is important to list.
- Software programs in which you are proficient.

The following tips should guide your selection of jobs you list on your résumé:
- Mention all design jobs, but listing unrelated employment is largely a waste of space and time.
- Be sure to have a portfolio sample from each design job you list—if you don't, it's apt to seem suspicious. The omission indicates that either you failed to produce work you were proud of or that the employer didn't have confidence in you. If you are too embarrassed to present a sample, it may be better not to mention the job on your résumé.

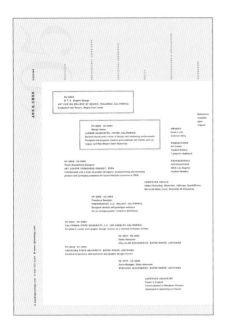

Ann Chen's résumé makes use of a subtle two-color background. In addition, she has simplified the information by separating it into different planes; category heads read vertically and body copy zigzags down the page in boxes. Although this design sounds chaotic, it is easy to navigate and illustrates Chen's understanding of information design.

Michelle Kim has an elegant résumé. With a narrow paper size of 7 ³⁄₈" × 11" (18.7 × 27.9 cm), it fits neatly into an art director's résumé file, but stands out from the competition. Headers, which are secondary to the information, run vertically to create another plane. To maintain consistency and make a personal statement, Kim uses a simple red string logo throughout her portfolio presentation (see pages 124–125).

Marina Chestnakova created a résumé with a simple and classic design. Two columns, one flush right and the other flush left, unjustified, organize the headings and other information nicely. This layout also establishes a strong asymmetrical vertical axis in the left third of the page. It's printed on heavyweight white paper and features a personal logo that is distinctive without being intrusive.

Jenna Talbott also makes use of two columns in her résumé, one flush right and the other flush left. The skewed columns suggest motion and keep the design from becoming static and dull. Talbott features the information and her name, while the headings remain secondary.

interface
The difficulty of creating computer animation on systems using command line interfaces helped to focus Paul's attention on the need for graphical user interfaces. In 1982 he contributed to the design of a program visualization environment sponsored by the Defense Advanced Research Projects Agency. This work led to additional user interface consultation for Computer Corporation of America, Javelin and Lotus.

computer animation
While he designed widely in print and managed many large print projects including books, at WGBH Paul also gained expertise in video design and production, frequently using innovative computer animation. A notable achievement was the production of the show open for *NOVA* in 1981 using experimental computer graphics systems at the New York Institute of Technology.

video
In 1977, he moved to WGBH Boston, the PBS flagship station, where he spent sixteen years designing print, video and multimedia elements for programs including *Frontline, KnowZone, NOVA, The Ten O'Clock News, This Old House, War and Peace in the Nuclear Age* and WGBH on-air breaks and promotion.

print
Paul's experience in the field of communication design has grown from a firm foundation in traditional design methods and principles. Beginning in 1971 with a B.A. in Advertising Art from North Texas State University, he worked first in traditional advertising/design studio settings, moving into television in 1975 at KERA, the PBS station in Dallas. As Art Director he was responsible for set design as well as print and video.

portfolio @
www.perfectdesignsense.com

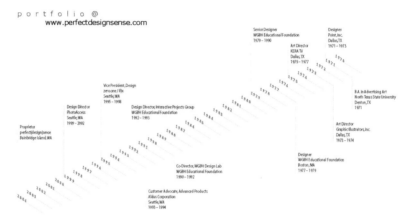

Paul has lectured extensively and has conducted many workshops on design, animation, interface, multimedia, computer graphics and video production. In 1994 he chaired the American Center for Design's *Living Surfaces: Interactive Media* conference.
His work has received numerous awards including gold medals from the Art Directors Club of Boston, Broadcast Designer's Association and National Association of Educational Broadcasters and the Grand Prize in Aldus Corporation's 1986 PageMaker Design Competition. His work has appeared in *Communication Arts, Graphis Annual, New York Art Directors Club Annual, AIGA Annuals, Print, Design Quarterly, Computer and IEEE Computer Graphics and Applications* and was selected for the 1984 SIGGRAPH Design Exhibition.
Paul has served as design consultant at the Photographic Resource Center and as founding art director of *Views, A New England Journal of Photography*. He was a member of the board of the American Center for Design, the Boston chapter of the American Institute of Graphic Arts and the Aldus Graphic Arts Advisory Board.

ABOVE
The ascending timeline in Paul Souza's résumé caught the attention of Chris Pullman at WGBH. This graphic tool is clever, effective, and memorable.

OPPOSITE
Two cover letters, one created before studying with Judith Aronson at Simmons College (left) and one after (right), demonstrate an improvement in design as well as content. The first letter has a designed heading but the text type is uninspired and the content is not as well composed. The second letter is elegant, consistent, and confident.

cover letters

- As with your résumé, your cover letter should be on high-quality paper, and designed in the same spirit, colors, and typeface as your résumé.
- It too must have perfect spelling and impeccable grammar. Topping the list for correct spelling is the name of the firm, the person you are addressing, and their correct title at the company, so take the time to confirm these details.
- As you write the body of your letter, be thorough, careful, and focused on the company you are addressing. Nonspecific flattery of a prospective employer is not as effective as referring to particular design you have seen and are familiar with. For example, if you are approaching a big corporation with the hope of designing their newsletter, take the time to review and even read the annual report. This will not only provide you with a better understanding of the company, it will give you a sense of their design aesthetic and give you something to discuss.
- In your cover letter, try to gently encourage the reader to look at your portfolio. It is important to impart a collaborative spirit and good work ethic; and as with interviews, avoid mentioning specific goals, lofty aspirations, or laying out "what I can do for you." This is not the place for strong opinions or mandates.

thank-you notes

Give careful thought to all follow-up materials, taking special care to make sure they reflect the interview. If an art director receives a common note card with a sentimental or meaningless message, the designer who sent it probably won't get the job. If the note is painfully gratuitous, it will seem insincere and potentially dishonest to an art director, but if it makes a clever connection to the interview, it will add to the applicant's appeal. In lieu of a note, it's also acceptable to send a grouping of work. Every personal initiative helps an employer gauge how committed the applicant is to good design. Thus, sending a CD by mail is more elegant and thoughtful than emailing a series of jpegs. A virtual presentation doesn't have the same presence as a physical object.

follow-up phone calls

When is it best to call as a friendly reminder that you want to work for a new client or secure a full-time position? For a staff job, one to two weeks is appropriate, depending on the timeline you were given at the interview. For freelance work, there is no rule of thumb so ask your client when the best time to contact them is. They probably receive many calls so your thoughtfulness will be appreciated.

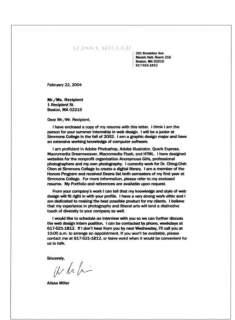

Promotions

mailers

Promotional pieces are in fact limited-edition portfolios that many professional designers distribute as reminders or enticements. They can be an effective means of catching and holding a client's attention. Often produced as little hand-bound books, they have a perceived permanence and personal appeal that keeps the art director or client from discarding them.

For Janet Odgis, who runs a design studio in Manhattan, promotional packets serve as both a follow-up to client meetings and a vehicle for informing existing clients about new projects. Her firm has found a simple and effective method for creating mailers. They select thirty-five work samples, create reduced images of them, and display them on a standard-size sheet of coated paper. A printer reproduces this one-sheet file in four-color process and trims the images into individual envelope-size cards measuring 7.5" × 4.75" (19.1 × 12.1 cm).

The printer punches one hole in the upper-left corner of each trimmed piece, so the internal design staff can insert a screw through the hole and make a fan of samples. This system provides a highly professional promo piece for relatively little money. Between certain pages, Odgis inserts a sheet of Mylar to offer brief pauses, or breaths, in the presentation. The entire mini-portfolio slips in a small bubble-wrap sheath and then in a padded mailing bag sealed with one of the firm's square mailing labels.

Sometimes, less expensive promotional pieces sometimes catch the most attention. A certain amount of roughness can indicate a designer or firm's ability to do innovative work without a big budget. London designer Milan Bozic's hand-made book falls into this category. Covered in red felt with a distinctive yellow heart on the front, the book includes samples of everything from books, billboards, and packaging to posters,

Odgis + Company's promotional piece fits perfectly inside a bubble-wrap sleeve and simple corrugated envelope. This inexpensive design choice is the perfect solution for their mailing.

Odgis + Company distributes this elegant promotional piece to existing and prospective clients. It has been printed commercially and has enough polish to catch the attention of big clients such as PriceWaterhouse-Coopers, Elizabeth Arden, and MoMA, but because it is hand-assembled in Janet Odgis' office and printed on only one sheet, it remains economical. The piece serves as a reminder portfolio to companies she is already acquainted with, as well as a method for showing new work to prospective clients.

logos, icons, and ideas. Because the book is playful but carefully crafted, art directors usually react positively, understanding that the artist is probably young and energetic—and probably affordable.

Another smart tactic is to pair a strong concept with exquisite production. As her first method of promotion, Louise Fili, a talented book and packaging designer, chose to design small letterpress books to display the logos she has designed for nearly every letter in the alphabet, packaging designs, and copyright page designs. Text precedes each image to explain the research and process behind the development of the design. To augment her design, Fili had the books printed at Stinehour Press and Dickson's, Inc., companies known for exceptionally high quality.

Perhaps a promotional piece's most important quality is an accurate reflection of the kind of work a designer wants to do. Roberto de Vicq de Cumptich, creative director at HarperCollins and designer of the children's book *Bembo's Zoo*, has made a lovely typographic book to promote his

design work. The small book, titled *Men of Letters*, depicts famous authors constructed from ornaments, dingbats, and alphabets, indicating de Vicq's interest in design work other than his primary specialty, book jacket design.

He printed 100 copies on a photocopy machine and sent them to several art directors, with no response. "Finally I showed [it] to a friend at Adobe, who liked it and asked me if I wanted to develop it as a promotional piece for Adobe InDesign," de Vicq says. "So I designed another book, *Words at Play*, for which I used one portrait from the original *Men of Letters*. All the fonts had to be in the Adobe font library, and all the writers had to have a quote that had the word *word* in it, and those quotes were the base to exemplify a feature of the InDesign software. To promote the book, a website was created, and to promote the website, I designed a little flipbook with two animations." Thus, de Vicq's charming little self-printed book helped him secure a prestigious and extended-contract design job.

Milan Bozic created this small 3.75" × 4.75" (9.5 × 12.1 cm) book by hand in his studio, complete with taped-in human hair. It primarily displays book jackets; packaging; logos; posters; and sassy, irreverent cartoons, all encased in a red felt cover. While it probably won't help Bozic land annual report jobs, the book's innovative and playful qualities are likely to grab an art director's attention.

Louise Fili uses these three exquisitely produced 4.25" × 6" (10.8 × 15.2 cm) paper-bound books as portfolios of her many restaurant logos; food-packaging designs; and copyright page designs, where the copy is formed into shapes that relate to the book's subject. Letterpress printing by Stinehour Press and Dickson's Inc. further enhances the classical and elegant presentation.

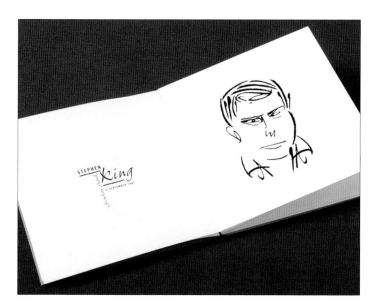

Roberto de Vicq de Cumptich's letterpress book, *Men of Letters*, is a exceptionally well-executed promotional piece showing portraits of famous authors that he created using typographic ornaments. Because it is an independent initiative separate from his work designing book jackets, it conveyed his interest in doing other types of design and landed him the high-profile job of creating InDesign promotional pieces.

Japanese designer Hirokazu Kurebayashi's promotional piece is noteworthy for its variety of
content. Like Janet Odgis' fan brochure, it is an
elegant professionally printed package for a corporate audience. It comes in a plastic sleeve that
opens to expose an outer cloth bag silk-screened
with the designer's name. The bag holds a four-
sided black cardboard envelope containing twenty-
seven printed samples. Each folded sample displays images showing Kurebayashis' design
process. Additionally, text printed on the back of
each card identifies the product and the client. It
is a collection of beautiful work, carefully printed
and packaged to enhance the presentation.

Hirokazu Kurebayashi's elegant promotional mailer comes in a simple black sack (opposite top). The first thing you remove is a 6 5⁄16" (16 cm) square envelope of black cardboard with his named stamped in white (opposite). The envelope opens on all four sides to reveal a stack of square printed pieces displaying a wide range of Kurebayashi's designs including books, fashion ads, water bottles, calendars, and swatch cards (above). Randomly interspersed are sheer pieces of Mylar offering a visual break (right).

Two Twelve Associates is a large New York–based design studio that produces identity work, signage, and various types of print communication. Because a large portion of the firm's work is signage for hospitals and universities, a website is the perfect vehicle for their portfolio. But websites are passive—you go to them rather than having them come to you—so they also send mailers, which play a more active role in reminding clients that they are available. Two Twelve's mailers are playful photographic references that feature recent work and illustrate the firm's specialty as sign and information designers.

Two Twelve Associates sends various postcard-size photos taken around the world, including photographs of street signs mailed in simple transparent wrappers that function as promotional reminders. The photographs remind clients of the firm's specialty in identity work and environmental design.

DESIGN FOR A BETTER EXPERIENCE™
www.twotwelve.com

2 12
TWO TWELVE
ASSOCIATES, INC.
902 BROADWAY
FLOOR 20
NEW YORK, NY
10010/6002
212 254/6670 T
212 254/6614 F

DAVID GIBSON
PRINCIPAL
dgibson@twotwelve.com

books and monographs

When a designer or design studio becomes highly successful, it is not uncommon to author a scholarly book on a single topic or self-publish a book of their own work, which is called a monograph. These are often lovely creations, carefully designed and beautifully manufactured under the watchful eye of the designer. Like a portfolio, these books show the best examples of a designer or firm's work, along with works in progress and any influences that may be part of the creative process. Sometimes, designers even include photographs of themselves in their studios or interacting with their families as a way of personalizing the piece.

The design studio is in full control of every detail of the presentation, including format, content, order of elements, design, paper, and printing. The books are distributed thoughtfully to prospective clients, and occasionally are sold in bookstores or online. The only problem with published monographs is that they tend to send the message that the design studio is expensive and that only large, profitable corporations can afford them.

These books are expensive, time-consuming, and difficult to sell because the market is so limited. In general, the average graphic design book buyer is looking for collections of work from a variety of designers rather than a single firm. Therefore, publishing such a book is not an option for all design studios but only for the limited few who can justify the production expense with guaranteed sales or who are profitable enough to cover the expense.

Logo, a design group in Uruguay, decided to develop a self-promotional brochure about their city, Montevideo. The piece, titled *Lovetour*, takes the viewer on a tourist's itinerary through the city while showcasing Logo's design skills.

TOP
Chen Zhengda, one of China's most talented poster
designers, produced this stunning promotional book
wrapped in an intense shade of salmon that continues
inside on the endpapers. Page after page, this exquisite
book contains an array of his beautifully designed work.

ABOVE
"Tasting War" is a powerful anti-war poster featured in
Chen Zhengda's book.

These two posters by Chen Zhengda analyze the
relationship between an ancient Chinese geometric
symbol and the regular patterns of standardized contemporary graphics on the occasion of Spring Festival.

Another beautiful poster in Chen Zhengda's book.

Min Wang's main portfolio is a beautiful hardcover book. In addition to being dean of the Central Academy of Fine Arts in Beijing, China, he is an active member of the design group Square Two and has designed extensively for Adobe. Currently, he is designing the signage for the upcoming Olympics in China. The 5" × 12.25" (12.7 × 31.1 cm) book alternates between English and Chinese text, and displays images of his posters, logos, and product packaging, as well as photos of his mentors.

Thonik, a design studio in Amsterdam, produced a bold orange, glossy book to promote the firm's work (left). Inside the book is a display of intensely bright graphics that often feature startling combinations. A simple sans-serif type, for example, is superimposed on images of classical Dutch oil paintings (below). This monograph not only features Thonik's book designs, ads, and posters, but also shows the designers working and exhibiting their work. According to the studio, the overall message is to "design without style and with a minimum of form. If the concept is good, the rest follows naturally."

CDs

When a live presentation is not an option, you can send electronic files to an art director on a CD. Because you send them by mail rather than email, they are less intrusive than a PDF. CDs are also small and easy for art directors to store for future reference. Both CDs and PDFs offer the potential to show work unadorned, as a product shot, or with text to accompany a design. One feature that makes CDs more attractive is that the colors may be a more accurate as PDFs sometime appear to be slightly muted.

PDFs

Designers who need to send electronic files of their portfolios via the internet or on a CD often create them as PDFs (portable document format.) This is a good choice because many program files can be captured in this format including Quark, InDesign, Photoshop, and Illustrator. The program compresses the documents into files small enough to email, and those viewing the PDF don't have to worry about having the right software because essentially the PDF is a snapshot of the document. PDFs are extremely easy to make, easy to update, and much less expensive than a website of your work. On the receiving end, the software used to read the files is free and highly available. PDFs have become the digital portfolio format of choice for designers all over the world because they are a quick and simple tool for promoting design work.

The cover of this mini CD was designed by a student at Massachusetts College of Art. The case was originally presented as an alternative compact size but was later discontinued due to the fact that it jammed when inserted in many laptops. When sending electronic files, it is wise to choose a known format that is predictable over a novelty that may fail or worse, cause damage. A well-designed package on a promotional CD is another detail that shows design initiative.

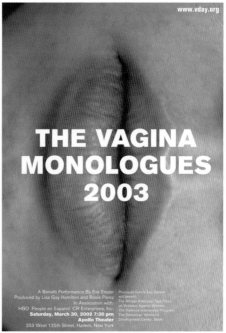

This poster was designed by Sagi Haviv, an Israeli designer in the new studio of Chermayeff & Geismar. While a student at Cooper Union, he was offered an opportunity to design a poster for the now-famous play *The Vagina Monologues*. Although this poster is simple and effective, it was considered too provocative to use.

An important thing to remember when emailing PDFs is the size of the file. As a rule of thumb, five megabytes will ensure the document is able to navigate successfully through an Internet connection.

Sagi Haviv, who works for Chermayeff & Geismar Studio in New York, currently has no need for a print portfolio. His philosophy is that the work should stand on its own, so he offers clients PDF files of his designs. Because his work is largely poster design, which can be cumbersome to present full size, and logo design, which works as well on screen as it does in person, this simple electronic format is a good alternative. Haviv's method, however, is a risky choice for less established designers who would do better to choose a more traditional and formal presentation or for

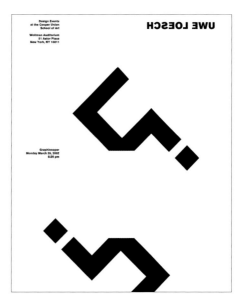

In this poster, Haviv dissected the swastika, separated the pieces, and used them to form two question marks. The piece announces a lecture by Uwe Loesch, a German graphic designer who examines the Nazi legacy in his country.

Haviv's poster announces a lecture by Leonardo Sonnoli, an Italian type designer who often creates three-dimensional letters. Designed in the colors of the Italian flag, the poster communicates the subject of the talk using a cube of letters as an analogous graphic symbol.

"Less Is More" is another clever poster designed by Haviv for the Uwe Loesch lecture series at Cooper Union. Haviv has erased certain letters of the phrase *postmodern design*, leaving only shadows and the word *more* intact.

designers who work with publications or special production techniques.

George Restrepo, a Boston-based designer, also uses PDFs to advertise his work. To complement the images of his designs, he includes a page or more of text in the PDF. His promotional PDF *New Work*, for example, displays four *Boston Review* cover designs adjacent to a page featuring a quotation by noted economist John Kenneth Galbraith: "*Boston Review* operates at a level of literacy and responsibility which is all too rare in our time." Like a blurb on a book jacket, this quotation gives Restrepo's work an air of authority.

GARRISON INSTITUTE

ABOVE
In Haviv's logo design for a New York State Buddhist retreat, he used the endless knot, one of the eight auspicious symbols of Buddhism, and highlighted a *G* for the Garrison Institute within the design. Because this is one of the most widely recognized symbols in Buddhism, it is a perfect logo for the retreat.

PUBLICATION DESIGN

"Consciousness implies choice, and thus the self is freedom: 'the more consciousness, the more self; the more consciousness, the more will…
—*Scott O'Leary, excerpt from Sin, Despair, and the Other: The Works of Soren Kierkegaard*

ELEMENTS, BOSTON COLLEGE UNDERGRADUATE RESEARCH JOURNAL

Elements, Boston College's first and only undergraduate research journal, was founded in September 2004 by a group of twenty undergraduate students. The journal published its first issue in May of 2005, featuring research articles written by BC undergraduates along with shorter special features.

The goal of the publication is to become a forum for the exchange of original ideas within and across disciplines at the university. This publication needed to stand out among the rest of the journals that other competeating institutions have been producing.

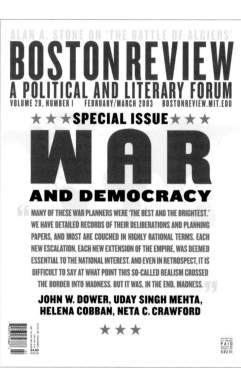

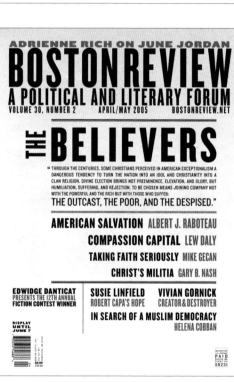

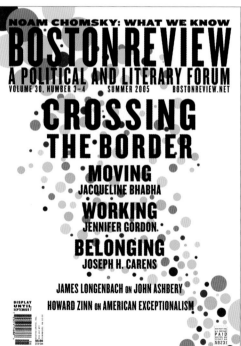

ABOVE and OPPOSITE
Designer George Restrepo's promotional PDF includes images of these four dynamic typographic *Boston Review* covers. The images are paired with a quote from Soren Kierkegaard, shown opposite, which illuminates the magazine's core values.

Some designers, such as Eric Cruz at Wieden+ Kennedy in Japan, think print portfolios are a thing of the past. Because most design students have portfolios that contain both print and electronic media, Cruz finds less and less justification for traditional portfolios. He believes that very few students produce print work and that if they do, it can be presented just as effectively as a PDF. When Cruz graduated from the University of California, he created a custom soft case to house prints and slides of his work, as well as books. But, he says, these days most students that he comes across skip the traditional presentation and let great work speak for itself. In his opinion, the work inside many elaborate portfolios doesn't live up to the packaging.

ABOVE
Eric Cruz, who works for Wieden+Kennedy in Japan, believes that print portfolios are a thing of the past. He emails PDFs displaying skillfully art-directed product photos of his CDs to clients and art directors all over the world. This is a sample image from one of his PDFs.

OPPOSITE
This poster called "Headless Faith" was part of Cruz's graduate thesis at Cranbrook Academy of Art. Cruz sends this as additional material with his CD designs to show a wider range of work.

Nike Presto "Instant Go"

W+K Tokyo is about creative collaborations. Here new post-grafitti generation artists from New York, Tokyo and Hong Kong work with top young digital artists from Los Angeles and an influential young Tokyo DJ to inspire people to be instantly active through Nike Presto shoes.

THIS PAGE
Eric Cruz's electronic portfolio contains a PDF that displays a page of text opposite an image of his design for Instant Nike Presto Shoes. The copy tells viewers that the art was a collaboration between postgraffiti generation and digital artists. This DVD was originally created for core influencers—such as DJs and artists—but it was so popular that it was eventually given away at Nike's Tokyo concept shop with shoe purchases.

OPPOSITE
Cruz's portfolio includes CD packaging for Japanese music labels; he sends shots of the products in PDF format. It's a quick and easy way to let potential clients view his work.

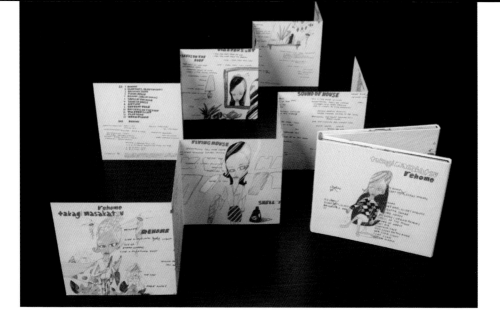

Creating Interactive Portfolios and Websites

For many design jobs, websites are the first place an art director will view a designer's work; the designer then needs to follow up with a print portfolio and live presentation. But for website designers, motion video designers, and product designers, websites are the best and, sometimes, only meaningful way to show their work. Online portfolios, however, aren't just for tech-heavy design. They are also a great way to display any piece that would need to be photographed for inclusion in a traditional print portfolio—everything from food packaging and outdoor signage to large three-dimensional objects.

Because websites can be viewed at any time of the day or night, they can be a particularly effective way of ensuring that your work gets seen. Many clients expect successful professional designers to have a website. It's a sign that a designer is established and serious about his or her work. Websites have also eliminated many international barriers to business by reducing the need to send print portfolios between countries.

Many successful design studios redesign their sites as often as once a year to maintain a good reputation and stay current. Websites also need to be updated frequently to show recent work and give viewers a reason to come back. In general, firms or individual designers hire a Web designer or programming specialist to create a site and work closely with them on the overall concept and function. It's important that a website match the tone and style of the work of the designer or design firm.

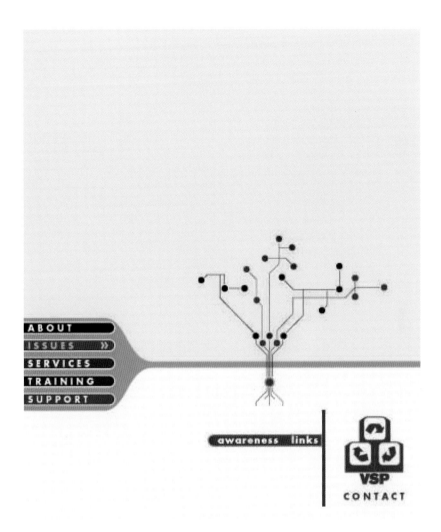

ABOUT

ISSUES »

SERVICES

TRAINING

SUPPORT

awareness links

VSP

CONTACT

ABOVE
Nathan Zarse, a student from the Herron School of Art
and Design, displays his interest in 1950s design on his
website. He gives it a period look and theme by using a
palette of pale green and cream and setting the text in
letterspaced sans-serif type.

OPPOSITE
A playful, interactive design by Zarse on this Web page
instructs the viewer to choose paint colors that brighten
spirits, ease tension, or enlarge space.

web portfolios and job hunting

There are two ways potential employers evaluate Web portfolios. First, they consider the material the site is showing them, and then, the site itself. "If a website takes too long to load, if it's a mile wide and an inch deep, if it's hard to navigate, cumbersome, or corny, that's bad," says Chris Pullman of WGBH. "A website can be a dangerous proposition. A Web designer doesn't know by which method people are viewing it. Viewers can be on a dial-up line or have sophisticated flash software. A website should therefore have two or even at times three options, one for people with flash, one for those without, and one for people with only simple HTML."

The first thing Pullman looks for in a website is a good range of work and an overview of the designer's accomplishments. He wants to understand the types of media the designer has worked with and see both small- and large-scale work, in terms of both physical size and clients. A Web portfolio should include a healthy number of samples, and Pullman likes to see a wide range of subjects. It also helps to give context to individual samples. What was the problem? And how was it solved? These questions can easily be answered with small blocks of text that accompany each piece.

pros and cons

For designers who specialize in areas such as book design, annual reports, and information design, a website is a less effective way of presenting a portfolio. It is virtually impossible to thoroughly review typography and printing quality on a website, so in some cases the online portfolio should serve only as a visual preview or advertisement, not a finished presentation. The bottom line, however, is that a website is expected and even required in today's marketplace. Therefore, it is important to be as thorough in designing it as in designing your print portfolio.

One benefit of a Web portfolio is its potential to function as a work archive—a technique that Lorraine Wild uses effectively in the website for Green Dragon Office of Los Angeles. The site documents books produced from 1994 to 2004 in a clear, systematic way that shows off the depth of the firm's experience. Because some years have been more prolific than others, it's a somewhat risky proposition, but the overall effect of the site is stunning. The quantity of books is so great that Wild and her three partners could never attempt to haul them around to interviews.

To make the site more informative, Green Dragon Office has created three motion films that show a hand turning the pages of beautifully designed art books. This presentation method simultaneously conveys the scale and pace of each book and makes the texts resemble moving pictures. In essence, the books make an impact via the series of linked images—more than they would with images of one or two sample spreads. These films duplicate the sensation of leafing through an entire book and are a perfect way to display complex work online.

One final benefit of websites is that they allow a designer to assemble and organize a diverse body of work in a more cohesive way than is possible with a print portfolio. If the work is separated into categories, such as logos, corporate, and personal work, viewers can find exactly what they are looking for and get a better sense of the designer's style in each area.

issues to consider

If they are not well designed, websites can be a risky first impression on several levels. Because there is no way to control what path a viewer will take to explore individual pages, it's extremely important to create a site that's strong throughout. Technology can be a hurdle; even the best site becomes ineffective when the viewer has an older computer or a slow Internet connection. To offset this problem, some sites start with a "landing page" that allows visitors to select whether to view a version designed for high-speed connections or a simpler, pared-down site for dial-up connections. Finally, websites have a tendency to be cool and impersonal. Many companies, such as Two Twelve Associates in New York and Group 94 in Belgium, combat this problem with friendly shots of staff meetings or design principals.

The first step is choosing an appropriate layout and structure for a site. Do you want to use a grid system or try a less traditional approach? How many layers of content do you need? Where will you place the menu? What items will be included on the menu? Peter Lehman, Web designer at WGBH and a Web design teacher at the Art Institute of Boston, gives the following advice: Never make a website so complicated that it takes over someone's browser.

Instead, he suggests making a site in which it is impossible to get lost by setting up a menu incorporating icons for easy navigation. Dividing the content on the site into logical items on the menu will also help viewers find what they need quickly. One of Lehman's students, Lucas Walker, created a splash page that follows these guidelines. While the design is simple and easy to navigate, it still succeeds in projecting Lucas's interest in illustration.

When working out the details of their sites, many designers write text to explain how they developed specific designs. This simple addition gives site visitors a glimpse into the thought process behind the work, offering the samples additional context and meaning. New York– and Los Angeles–based design firm Imaginary Forces,

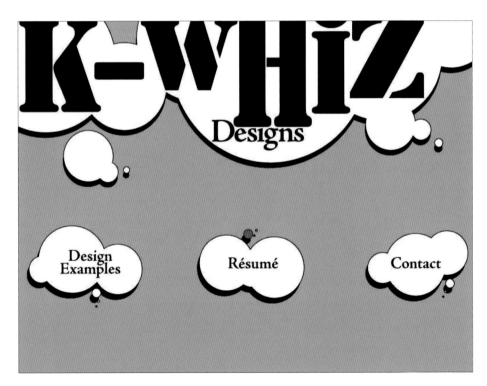

Lucas Walker, a student at the Art Institute of Boston, created this simple, easy-to-navigate splash page. As a designer, he gravitates toward illustration, so he chose to use sky and cartoon speech bubbles as the vehicle for his opening page.

LOUISE FILI LTD

FOOD PACKAGING | LOGOS | RESTAURANTS | *books* | BIO/CONTACT

1 2 3 4 5 6 7 8 **9** 10 11 12 13 **ITALIAN ART DECO**

ORDER THIS BOOK

LOUISE FILI LTD

FOOD PACKAGING | LOGOS | *restaurants* | BOOKS | BIO/CONTACT

1 2 3 **4 5** 6 7 8 9 10 11 12 13 14 15 16 17 **PACE**

for example, includes explanatory text within the portfolio section of its website. Interactive ads for the Honda Element are paired with text that explains the overarching concept behind the design: "In these short films, the four elements—Fire, Water, Earth, and Air—are seen as a metaphor for human sensation and thought."

when is a website enough?

In some cases, a website may be the only portfolio a designer or studio needs to find work. This is especially true for interactive designers, but it also extends to other disciplines. Photographer and designer Tom Wedell, for example, says that many of his photo clients see enough work on his website to hire him. Photographs, particularly color ones, reproduce well online. As noted earlier in the PDF section, a good rule of thumb is that any sample which relies on photos for presentation within a print portfolio will translate well online. This might include food packaging, product design, restaurant menus, and signage.

Louise Fili, famous for her book design and restaurant identities, has created an elegant website that performs as a portfolio with amazing success. Because so much of her work is product-based—ranging from restaurant signs and menus to pasta packages and cracker tins—a print portfolio is an awkward proposition. To solve the problem, Fili worked with Maine-based Web designer Tom Morgan to create a well-designed, easy-to-use site that perfectly reflects her style. Viewers can quickly navigate to images of Fili's work through four categories, each of which contains roughly sixteen designs. As the user rolls over a line of numbers, the name of each project appears to the right of the list. The only problem Fili must contend with is that much

of her work is related to restaurants—a segment in which businesses open and close quickly. As a result, she has to remove designs from her site when a client shuts the doors to avoid having her work associated with failure.

music

Like most art forms, music is highly subjective. There's nothing worse than logging onto an attractive website and not being able to figure out how to turn off an irritating sound track. Since music taste is extremely personal, it's difficult to predict the reaction of users. For this reason, many designers aren't in favor of adding music to websites. Television commercials, however, often use nostalgic music to great advantage. What makes the difference? Unlike a television, a computer is often in a workplace and sound can be an unexpected—and unwanted—surprise. If you decide music enhances the overall site presentation, be sure the off button is easy to find.

Music for its own sake doesn't appeal to Chris Pullman of WGBH. In most cases, he will turn it off. Music puts a viewer in a certain zone, and if the listener doesn't like the music, it has an adverse effect. At Kyle Cooper's studio, Prologue, the feeling is that music with websites is inherently problematic. The user is in complete control of navigating the website, so there is no way to edit or control the sound track to be sure the viewer is hearing the music in relationship to the corresponding images. Cooper thinks that even the option of music on a website can be distracting and risky.

A book and a restaurant sign from Louise Fili's website (www.louisefili.com) show the amazing facility of interactive design to unify diverse pieces— things that may be designed in the same spirit but can make awkward bedfellows in a print portfolio.

Motion Graphics and Broadcast Design Portfolios

In some respects, a connection exists between motion graphics and broadcast design portfolios and poster or book jacket design. In both cases, the designer is distilling a select group of images or ideas into a potent single set that represents the larger work. But whereas poster and book jacket designs are static, motion portfolios introduce time, multiple images, and often sound to add a richer, but also temporary, effect. You can't sit and stare at a motion portfolio indefinitely. By definition, it's a presentation that comes to an end.

These portfolios, which are generally provided on VHS, CD, or DVD, vary in length. Most have music to accompany them because sound is such an essential part of this area of design. The range in content is tremendous and can include anything from commercials and architectural films to more esoteric subjects such as people and relationships. Additionally, there are movie portfolios, such as one from Kyle Cooper of Prologue, who produces title sequences and television openers. His clip features movie stills, movie stars, and advertising clips in rapid succession. These film portfolios are often one minute long at most and are carefully composed to get the most visibility and recognition in a short span.

According to Kyle Cooper, one of the major challenges with a motion portfolio is linking the visual aspects of the reel. With so many images flying around the screen, it can be difficult to find consistent themes. If you can transition from second to second with some system of commonality, such as shapes, colors, or angles, it helps make a smooth reel. What Cooper does best is what is common to most design: he systematically removes everything that does not fit, leaving the core idea. This involves editing and reviewing countless hours of content. "When you realize that that two-minute reel is your identity, you take a lot of care in creating something that represents you as an artist in as many lights as possible," he says.

But motion portfolios are not only designed to feature motion work; some choose to animate still work to great effect. As part of a traveling exhibit named Designing over Four Decades, Ivan Chermayeff, Tom Geismar, and Steff Geissbuhler worked with Sagi Haviv, who created a film called *Logomotion*. One by one, sixty-seven logos and trademarks designed by Chermayeff & Geismar Inc. disassemble, morph, and reform in a seamless flow of imagery to a perfect soundtrack of bells, drums, animal noises, and street sounds, composed by Shay Lynch. When developing a logo, a designer typically investigates the core meaning or function of a company, and develops the final mark by drawing, cropping, and exploring negative and positive space. This beautiful nine-minute film illustrates the process of exploration and development, and shows Chermayeff & Geismar Inc.'s extensive body of work in a piece that is a joy to watch.

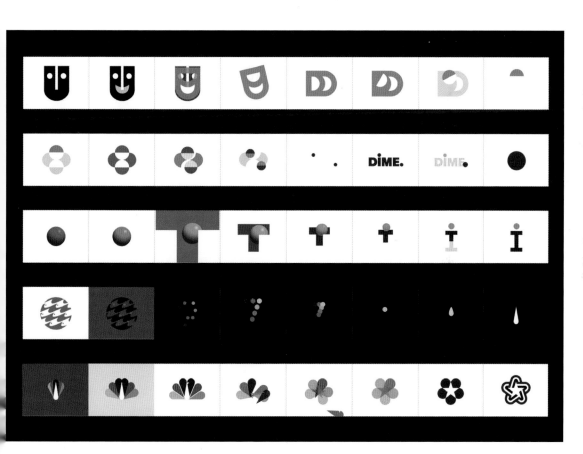

As part of a traveling exhibit, Designing over Four Decades, Ivan Chermayeff, Tom Geismar, and Steff Geissbuhler worked with Sagi Haviv, who created a film called *Logomotion*. This portfolio film hints at the process of development as each logo is cleverly formed from the one preceding it. The accompanying music, composed by Shay Lynch, gives the viewer further clues about the ideas and thoughts influencing the design. The film reminds us that logos are the synthesis of ideas.

THINGS TO CONSIDER Motion portfolios are exciting and complex newcomers to the world of design, but as with all new technology, there are challenges. It's essential that the client have compatible and up-to-date software and equipment so that the work can be presented smoothly—without interruption or painful pauses. If the equipment is problematic, the designer is suddenly in freefall, having failed to exhibit his or her work in a seamless presentation. One way to avoid this is to call ahead and inquire about the equipment or software available at the interview site. If you are presenting the work in person, it is best to bring your own laptop so you can avoid any technological variables.

The good news is that free plug-ins for Flash, the most common program for viewing motion work, are free and easy to download from the Web. This means that a client who doesn't have Flash software installed can quickly install it to view your motion portfolio. It's important, however, to do the research before choosing to employ new technology, because if something is very new, it's inherently inaccessible.

More and more, students are learning to make these works in design classes and may offer sample CDs with their print portfolios, résumés, cards, and other promotional giveaways to prospective clients. One such CD was sent to me from the graduating class of 2004 from Central Saint Martins College of Art and Design in London as a presentation of work from a motion graphic class. Because motion pieces are often collaborative by nature, the most important thing is to be clear about your role in the pieces featured in your presentation. For example, you might note that you designed the opening titles or provided the cinematography. On that same note, your résumé should also give a clear indication of what area of Web or motion design you specialize in. In selecting material for a motion portfolio, diversity is most important, because your reel is your calling card. You want to prove to the client you can produce many different kinds of projects.

ABOVE
Students at Central Saint Martins, Adrien Pelletier and Ladan Anousfar, made this wonderful motion portfolio piece. It uses dance as a metaphor for the intense emotion of a courtship.

OPPOSITE
Mats Dahle, also from Central Saint Martins College of Art and Design in London, created a virtual tour of a fencing academy for his motion portfolio. The motion video takes the viewer through the academy, while showing the details of the building and how the occupants function within the inner spaces.

SOUND CONSIDERATIONS While absent from most Web design, music is a common and important element of motion portfolios because it helps make these short presentations exhilarating to watch. Cooper says the main purpose of a reel is to dazzle the client and show the diversity of your portfolio. Because it is impossible to know exactly what a client is looking for, it's necessary to link dozens of blink-fast images together into a cohesive film—and music can be the consistent element that holds everything together, with the rhythm becoming a backbone. Soundtracks with a high number of beats per minute, such as techno or electronic soundtracks, are the most effective way to complement fast-moving visual material.

THE RIGHT LENGTH Motion portfolios tend to be short, often slightly less than one minute long. Kyle Cooper says there is no magic running time for Web-based motion portfolios. The most important thing is that the reel conveys your abilities. In general, Cooper recommends making a reel concise and simple, no longer than a few minutes. Clients are busy, so you want to show them your work quickly and not give them time to become bored. If you do special effects for film, then you might need to hold shots longer.

PREVIEWS Some designers create previews to their motion design portfolios, similar to intros on a website. Almost like preludes to musical scores, these short compositions are made up of tiny segments of material linked to introduce or persuade viewers to continue watching. Chris Pullman has seen many such previews at WGBH and admits that "there seems to be a knee-jerk method of making a preview, which is a compilation of the best two and a half seconds of work the designer has done." Generally, a hard rock or soft jazz soundtrack accompanies the preview. Pullman confesses that he fast-forwards past these first few seconds to the main piece. He wonders what the context of the preview is, and ultimately what it accomplishes since it does not give him any way of determining the competence of the designer.

BELOW
Crista Hirzel, a recent graduate of Massachusetts College of Art, shows this graphic motion portfolio piece called *Culture Tap* as part of her presentation. *Culture Tap* is a dynamic piece about the need to save water, making its case by showing all manner of nonwater objects, such as boots, hearts, and letters, coming from a faucet, whose handles carry images of Earth. A rhythmic soundtrack enhances the drama of the piece.

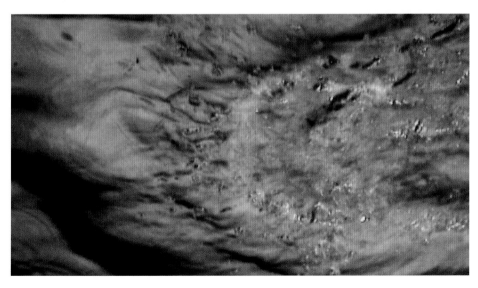

This portfolio piece, created by Holly Horner, another recent graduate of Central Saint Martins, shows swimmers moving through a pool, photographed with an underwater camera.

PART II

Gallery of Portfolios

Portfolios
That Got Jobs

Chip Kidd

In 1986, I was art director of book jackets at Alfred A. Knopf and needed an assistant. As a new graduate of Pennsylvania State University, Chip Kidd brought in a portfolio with two pieces that caught my attention. His presentation was more a series of posters than formal text treatments, and I was attracted to his talent and his daring page design. The first book he showed was made mostly from common construction paper. On the cover, in huge wood-type letters, were the words *Bippity Bangity Boppity*. As a whimsical visual interpretation of various percussion instruments found in marching bands, the book included an astounding variety of design techniques: die cuts, letterpress printing with large wood type, airbrush type, collage, foldouts, silk screening, and illustration.

The second book in his portfolio, which was equally ambitious, featured airbrush type, illustration, handwritten headline type, foldouts, photography, and images of cigar wrappers and

ABOVE
This page in Kidd's portfolio book uses wood type to spell out the sounds of a drum. Because the type and the implied sound are so large, Kidd incorporated foldouts to give the type more room.

RIGHT
Chip Kidd brought this handmade book about drumming with him for his first interview, and it stood out for several reasons. Made long before computers were used for graphic design, it showed examples of airbrush, illustration, die cuts, and mezzotints as well as items in his eclectic collections.

other collected art. Kidd had painstakingly created all of these special effects with antiquated equipment in those precomputer days. I was looking for a fresh designer, someone who wasn't overly influenced by popular trends. Kidd's willingness to mix mezzotints with shaded line drawings, collections of cigar wrappers, photographs, formal texts in French and German, and scratchy informal handwriting immediately caught my attention. At the same time, in spite of its incredible daring, his work had a formal quality to it. The images were bold, irreverent, and noisy while at the same time rhythmic and well paced.

In each book, Kidd also chose a subject that was meaningful to him—drumming and his passion for collecting common everyday things. But of all the parts that caught my attention, his illustrations were the most powerful. I told him the drawings reminded me structurally of Fernand Leger. Twenty years later, I might say a merger of cartoons and Leger. Either way, his portfolio was extraordinary.

The short pages shown here progress to wider pages, creating an amazing visual effect. Behind each illustrated face is a mezzotint face, which shows the transformation of the illustrated image to the final printed image.

In a separate magazine portfolio piece, Kidd
exhibits his passion for collecting by including
images of cigar wrappers and an assortment
of everyday vernacular objects.

Jim Drobka

A graduate of the California Institute of the Arts, Jim Drobka had one particular piece in his portfolio—the so-called fish book—that single-handedly landed him a job with the design department at the Los Angeles County Museum of Art. It's a simple burlap-covered book, wider than it is tall, with only a silhouetted fish on its front cover. The book opens with a poem, printed on two contrasting paper stocks: one transparent and the other brown opaque. The transparent sheet allows deliberate showthrough of image and text, reminiscent of traditional Japanese book design. This smoky layered effect evokes the sense of fish in water and expresses the dreamlike quality of the poem. To separate the text, Drobka used a combination of Trump Mediaeval and Univers.

From this beautiful book, Deenie Yudell, his creative director, was able to determine several things about Drobka. The most important was that he was a talented typographer who chose his faces thoughtfully and used them well. Yudell was also impressed by the ambitious project's complex layers, papers, and text-setting styles, including his decision to set phrases in sans serif type, which is quick and easy to read and draws in the readers' attention.

In many portfolios of young designers, the text is too small, gray, or dense to read, which almost never engages the viewer. If the reader can't easily read the text, then the meaning is lost. A nice image or photo with illegible or sloppy typography diminishes the impact significantly. When you look at Jim Drobka's fish book, however, you are invited to read it. The book's story takes place in the desert, so the horizontal format, tan paper, and rough burlap cover give a tactile sense of this expansive environment. One finishing touch, while minor, illustrates the designer's attention to detail: a colophon at the end identifies the typefaces, paper, and art.

ABOVE
Jim Drobka's final project at Cal Arts, the so-called fish
book, is printed on many different kinds of paper and
bound in burlap. It caught the attention of Deenie Yudell
at the Los Angeles County Museum of Art, who hired
him after seeing it.

BELOW
Some of the paper in Drobka's book is transparent,
imitating the murky water of the sea. All the typography
is high quality, highly legible, well kerned, carefully positioned, and in good scale and proportion. The excellent
typography caught Yudell's eye more than any other
feature of the book.

Will Staehle

Another example of a portfolio that helped secure a job is a book created by Will Staehle, now a book designer at HarperCollins. During his senior year at Minneapolis College of Art and Design, Staehle compiled his best student work into a book, which he had commercially printed in a limited edition. He produced six copies at a cost of $100 per copy and gave them to his biggest design heroes at an Adobe awards ceremony. The move landed him a job with one of those heroes, Roberto de Vicq de Cumptich at HarperCollins.

When Will Staehle graduated, he took a chance by spending $600 to produce six copies of a book containing some of his best work from school. Thankfully, his investment paid off when he landed a job with Roberto de Vicq de Cumptich at HarperCollins, one of the recipients.

Professional
Print Portfolios

Because Web-based portfolios are so convenient, print versions are becoming less common among design professionals and design studios. Still, I was able to find a number of professionals who had assembled print portfolios. Sometimes, a professional designer needs to present a portfolio when applying for a grant or award, such as the prestigious Cooper-Hewitt's National Design Award. Or a studio will keep a printed portfolio on hand in the event that a potential client requests it. Other designers, such as Kobi Benezri and Melle Hammer, create systems for quick-to-assemble and inexpensive giveaway portfolios. These efficient presentations are easy to update and can be sent two and three at a time if necessary.

Skolos-Wedell have an exceptional portfolio that's unique and well conceived. At first glance, it appears simple and classical: a handmade, cloth-covered case carefully designed to fit in a Federal Express box. Because it is covered with a textured gray fabric, the case can withstand slight scuffing, subtle fingerprints, and dings without immediately looking shabby. The firm pastes its business card onto a simple inset on the outside of the case—it's the only identifying feature and makes an elegant presentation. Tom Wedell prefers a classical case because it doesn't compete with the complex and extravagant work inside. In his opinion, "a fussy high-tech metallic presentation box would be overkill."

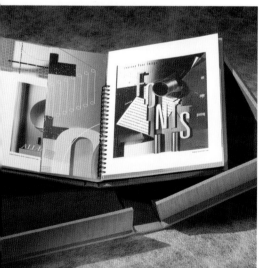

ABOVE
When opened, the case reveals a slim book bound in an identical gray fabric. Inside the book, canvas sleeves hold a removable spiral bound book containing pages produced on the studio printer. If the inner pages get damaged—or the designers want to include a slightly different body of work—the inner spiral bound book can be easily replaced.

LEFT
Skolos-Wedell are famous for their enormous posters, which measure approximately 3' × 4' (91.4 × 121.9 cm). This work constitutes a large portion of their portfolio, and the samples shown here have been reduced to fit the format. Two or three thumbnails are shown opposite each poster. They show the work in progress and are followed by one detail from each printed poster. This allows viewers to feel the texture of the stock, inspect the printing, and understand the original scale of the work.

Some of the pages in the book are half width while others are half height. With this barn-door effect, the viewer always sees the work in relation to the preceding and following pages.

This barn-door design solution, in which images are constantly put in new relationships with one another, reflects and enhances the process of Skolos-Wedell's complex design style. Elements integrate and reintegrate to make meaning. The look is chaotic and wonderful at the same time.

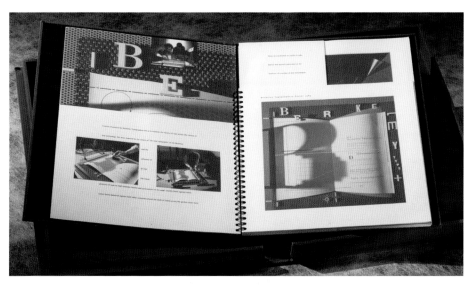

Stoltze Design's portfolio comprises specialized ring binder portfolios organized by subject. The idea behind having three portfolios is that certain clients prefer to see only specific segments of the studio's work, while others are more interested in seeing a broad range. Many big design firms maintain several portfolios and will even provide customized portfolios for a client. The first one, labeled Audiovisuals, shown opposite, bottom, features CD covers and boxes, logos, and general music industry materials. Because many of these materials are small, the ring binder is only 5.5" × 8.5" (13.4 × 21.6 cm).

PERSONAL WEB SITES

Book Cover
ROCKPORT PUBLISHERS
Personal Web Sites

PUBLICATION
FAST COMPANY MAGAZINE

CD packaging
HAYHOUSE / WINDHAM HILL
Series of 17 compilations

CD packaging
CASTLE VON BUHLER RECORDS
Relax + An art / music compilation

An art/music compilat

LEFT
The subject of the second binder, education, includes posters for schools as well as books and book covers.

BELOW and OPPOSITE
The third case is a larger, 8.3" × 13.5" (21.1 × 34.3 cm), silver aluminum case. This portfolio is more comprehensive, with sections titled Corporate, New Media, Publishing, Institutional, Entertainment, and Posters.

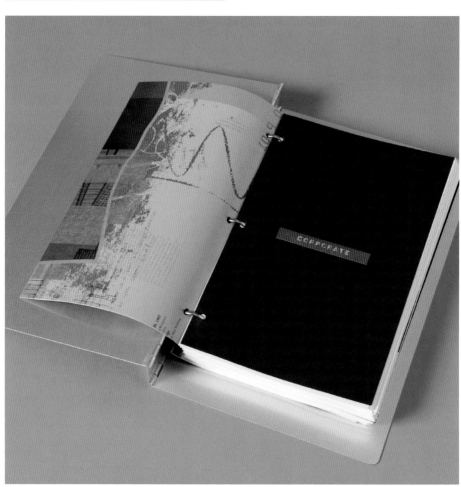

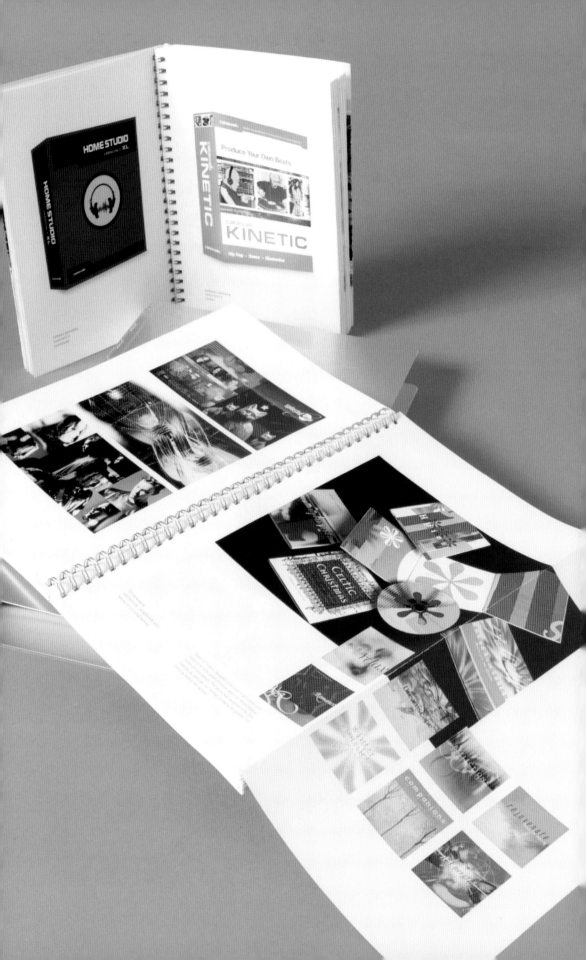

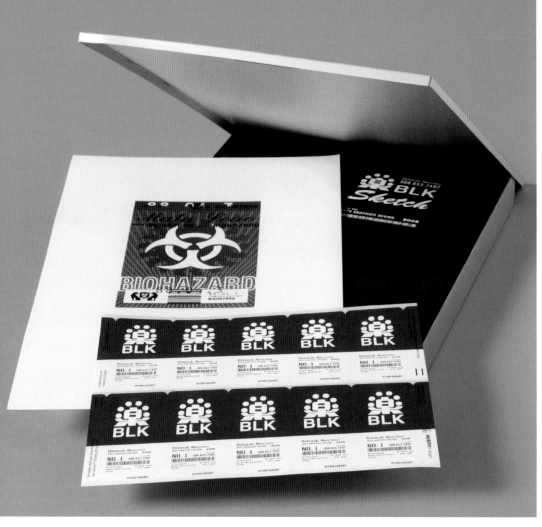

ABOVE
Deborah Norcross' portfolio is gathered from many years of recording industry work. For more than a decade, she produced exceptional CD designs at Warner Brothers by drawing from the influence of ticket stubs, hardware packaging, and an array of vernacular objects. Featured here is a jewel case and promotional piece for Mata Leao by Biohazard.

RIGHT
Norcross' portfolio is presented simply in a large book, which fits perfectly into an aluminum case, which in turn folds easily into a black canvas bag (not shown). The portfolio is not overdone, glittery, or expensive, but is professional and complete.

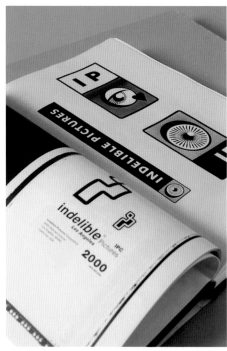

LEFT and BELOW
A promotional giveaway package printed by Norcross features many of her CD designs as well as other pieces she created for the music industry.

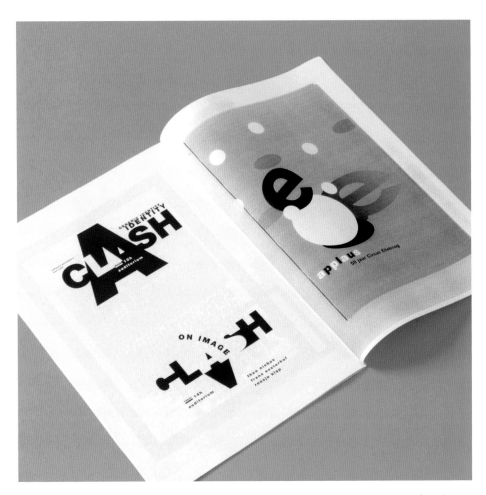

Melle Hammer, an extraordinary designer from the Netherlands, creates books, posters, opera sets, short films, tickets, invitations, logos, and even puppet theaters. In his words, "The moment I need a portfolio to introduce my work to a prospect, I give a general view of what keeps me busy, and show a series of similar projects (similar in subject or similar in the tools used)." This ensures that the content is always up to date and connected with the viewer's interests. Additionally, because a finished piece fails to communicate a project's budgetary or time constraints, he likes to explain the setting in which something was made whenever possible.

To create these custom portfolios, shown above and on page 107, Hammer makes black-and-white photocopies of selected images on inexpensive paper, puts it all together with a simple binding, and adds a short introduction. Its dimensions are 8.2" × 11.75" (21 × 29.8 cm), and despite the inferior reproduction quality, the work holds up. He likes to present design work without "seducing or polishing the parts."

Hammer created this poster announcing DesignInquiry 2003, "Off the Page," to attract designers to a week-long seminar at the Maine Summer Institute in Graphic Design.

LEFT and OPPOSITE
Hammer created an unbound book called *Klap* as a personal typographic exercise. He set himself the challenge of making a book using the single word *Klap* (Dutch for clap) to represent the physical soundscape of an applauding audience. Hammer produced this piece as part of an exhibition in France, not as a project for a specific client.

BELOW
Instead of keeping a single formal portfolio, he sends a selection of work specific to the client or type of design requested.

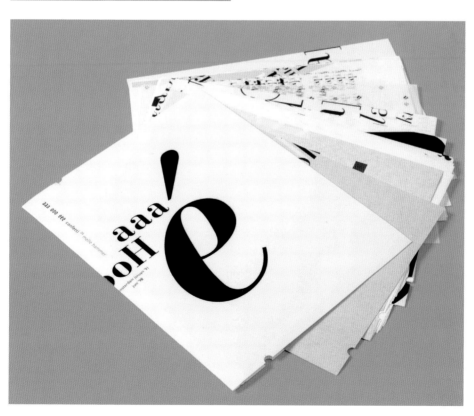

Rebeca Mendez, a designer and a professor at UCLA Design | Media, produced and presented this portfolio to the Cooper-Hewitt award committee. The collection includes her most recent work, which is largely brand research and reports for such companies as Mattel, IBM, Motorola, and UCLA. It also features her beautifully designed art catalogs for Bill Viola and the Art Center College of Design in Pasadena. Each year, several finalists receive the honor of being selected for the Cooper-Hewitt's National Design Award. Mendez gathered the materials she needed to show and found a box at the art store large enough to accommodate the work. The manufactured linen covered box worked perfectly because it is simple, well made, and not overly intrusive.

The International Design Magazine 2005 Annual Design Review featuring 150 winners

51st Annual Design Review

Consumer Products
Graphics
Packaging
Environments
Furniture
Equipment
Concepts
Interactive

I.D.

The International Design Magazine Emerging Talent ... New York ... London ... Groningen ... Moscow ... Cape Town ... Cambridge ... Student Design Review

I.D.

brilliant, they're dogcone it, people of today's young et any cooler.

tion

The International Design Magazine Introducing Design and Business: Bridging the Gap ....
Polar Adventure Gear ... World's Sexiest Motorcycle ... North Korea Style ...

I.D.

PROFILE OF
Alfredo Häberli

Getting to Know the
Swiss Design Star

"The magazine box intuitively communicates the printed materials it holds," says *I.D.* art director Kobi Benezri about his portfolio. "My hope is that it invites the viewer to interact with the portfolio as he might his own book-shelf, picking up pieces one at a time and judging them on their own merits."

ABOVE
Benezri sees distinct advantages with all print portfolios. "There's nothing like the real thing," he says. "When a client asks to see my work, I prefer to give him actual completed pieces. To handle graphic-design collateral is to understand it as a three-dimensional experience as well as a two-dimensional visual statement."

OPPOSITE
Benezri's solution also solved spatial problems. The magazines are substantially larger than his small bound school portfolio and, in addition, he planned to include a beautiful dummy currently being designed for a book on Frank Lloyd Wright. The magazine box accommodates all the pieces neatly, despite their different shapes and is perfectly appropriate for a designer who is primarily a magazine art director. For students, however, using a magazine box as portfolio could be too narrowly targeted.

Modern Dog is an irreverent and highly successful design group from Seattle. The firm's portfolio arrives unassembled in a FedEx box (above). A CD containing poster work, stills of old TV shows, CD designs for Lou Reed and the Pretenders, as well as gum packages, lip gloss, playing cards, a T-shirt, sheets of play stamps, and various books of logos and designs spilled out of the FedEx box (above and top). The effect is both outrageous and compelling.

ABOVE
Modern Dog created this custom-made portfolio for Adidas. In fact, custom-made, targeted promotional books, according to cofounder Robynne Raye, are the studio's single most successful means of attracting clients.

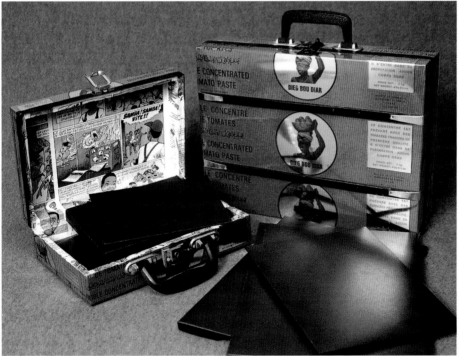

When describing her tin box portfolios from Africa, Robin Lynch says they are "made from cut-up coffee cans and lined in comics. When I need to present, I go shopping in my samples. Over the years, I have bought subcontainers to both homogenize and reign in the experience for the recipient. Sometimes, I include an annotated inventory." This approach offers her great flexibility in customizing presentations, which has been important for her practice, given its wide variety of clientele.

Student
Print Portfolios

Most graduating design students create print portfolios; they typically spend the last part of their senior year assembling all their best projects into a presentation box of some kind. Often, students will polish or rework old pieces and add some extra promotional work. Boxes are made or purchased to fit the material, both physically and stylistically. Frequently, the portfolio has a theme, as in the case of Rhode Island School of Design student Michelle Kim's white case with red string (124–125). She titled it "Being Green" to signal her newness in the field. Increasingly, student portfolios take the form of printed books, organized around a central idea that expresses the student's best.

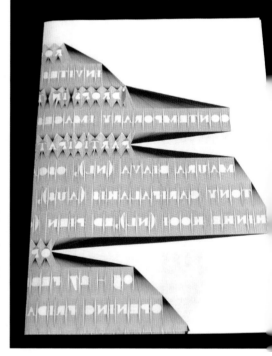

Hansje van Halem is a recent graduate of Gerrit Rietveld Academy in Amsterdam. Her portfolio consists of several jpegs displaying her design work. These electronic files come to art directors accompanied by a résumé that includes descriptions of the work. This page is from a flipbook called *Damp*. It's a conceptual exploration of the complexities of typography and typographic design. The design is part of Halem's graduation project.

An invitation commissioned by Room investigates the idea of available space. In Halem's words, "This piece works on the level of letter shapes instead of paper edges. Within the vertical and diagonal lines, the letter shapes are left blank."

The image shown here is an invitation that was commissioned for an artist-run space
called Room; it promotes a growing collection of artist publications called *Print Room*.
The physical space of the Room is symbolized by lines that stop at the edges of the title.

LEFT
This design by Halem is called *The Scratched Letter*. Here, she scratched or drew letterforms by hand; they become denser and fully black as the book progresses. Art directors might be drawn to this piece because of its in-depth exploration of typography. The sample also shows Halem's extraordinary drawing skills.

LEFT
As part of her thesis, Halem created this annual report for VPRO, a Dutch broadcasting company. It's a book inside a book, with random messages that pop up to brighten the report.

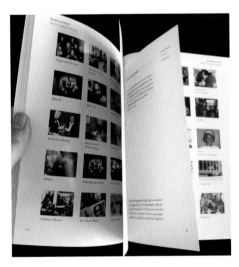

BELOW
The Thinking Forward Festival, a European cultural festival that celebrates the Dutch presidency, commissioned these books. Halem created two pieces that fold into an olive green cover. The pink booklet is a catalog of participants; the blue booklet contains text describing the festival. Halem's dignified and understated approach to the project shows art directors that she understands how to enhance, not overshadow, content with design.

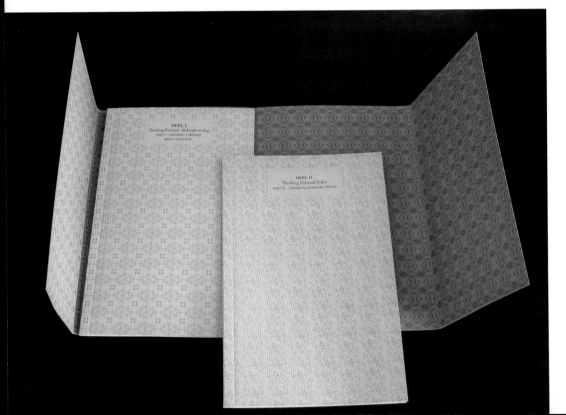

LEFT

Commissioned by the Stedelijk Museum in Amsterdam in 2004, this catalog is called *Municipal Art Acquisitions Graphic Design*. It has spots for eighty-four designs, but the sixty-four that didn't make the cut are represented by punched-out windows, leaving only the twenty final selections in place.

BELOW

Designed by Halem in cooperation with Gerard Unger for the City Council of Amsterdam, this report consists of information on Amsterdam Cultural Art Initiatives. It is a simple, elegant typographic report that's printed exceedingly well on thin paper. There's a subtle echo of text running down the outer and inner edges of each page for emphasis. The fact that Halem collaborated with such a well-known designer is one of the reasons this is such a strong portfolio piece.

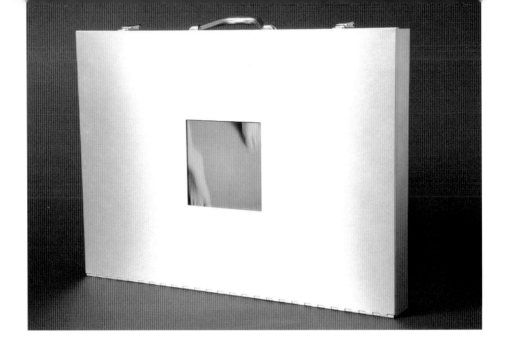

TOP
Crista Hirzel, a recent graduate of Massachusetts College of Art, has a
single large aluminum portfolio to hold her photography and design samples.

ABOVE
Since a large portion of her work addresses social responsibility and environmental
issues, Hirzel chose simple cardboard as her packing material to make an ecological
statement. She cut large shapes from plain corrugated cardboard to hold the various
design projects in place. A number of pieces—books, advertisements, and reduced-
size posters—are carefully positioned in the box and held in place by the cardboard
dividers. Separately, she carries large posters in cardboard sleeves as well as a laptop
computer for displaying items such as environmentally sensitive screen savers.

Perhaps the most elegant presentation in Hirzel's portfolio is her book of photographs, which uses an amazing shade of soft mauve for the type.

you leave water running while you brush your teeth, you waste **5** gallons of water, **2/3** of the people of the world use less than **13** gallons of water a day for all their needs.

LEFT (ALL)
On a CD in her portfolio, Hirzel includes three screen savers that promote her passion for environmental preservation. The first screen saver is a toothbrush with the message "IF" in large letters, reminding us not to waste water. The second, featuring a half-submerged porthole, speaks to greenhouse emissions and the last, a plugged in Coca-Cola can, is a reminder to recycle.

there is no reduction in greenhouse emissions, sea level will rise **20 cm** by the year **2030**.

you recycle just **1** aluminum can, you save enough energy to run a television set for **3** hours.

RIGHT and OPPOSITE
Hirzel successfully displays these two posters in her portfolio. The posters—against sex trafficking and female circumcision—are both subjects she is passionate about. They also fit well within her portfolio's theme of environmental responsibility and human rights.

Circumcision = Torture

No one shall be subjected to cruel and inhuman treatment UN Declaration of Human Rights Article 5

UN Declaration of Human Rights

No one shall be bought or sold

Sex trafficking equals slavery

ARTICLE 4

Hirzel, Crista, 2005

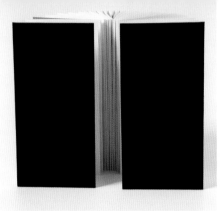 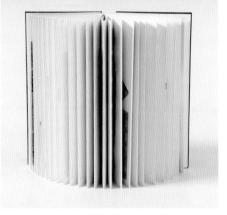

ABOVE (LEFT and RIGHT)
Hyun Auh is a graduate of FIT (Fashion Institute of Technology) in New York City. His portfolio is pure and economical, devoid of excess or decorative element. The dimension of his accordion-style portfolio is a sleek 5.5" × 11" (13.4 × 27.9 cm), and the book is housed in a simple cardboard case. Hyun is Korean, so the Asian-style binding and the order of contents have been designed in deference to his native country, where traditional books are read from back to front.

BELOW
This book includes reproductions of the work Auh created in four years of study. Typefaces are accompanied by process drawings, logos, books, and posters.

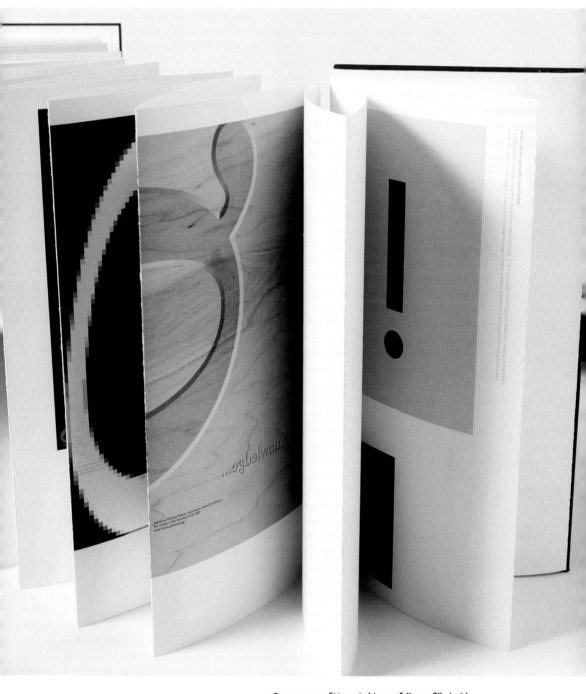

Some pages of Hyun Auh's portfolio are filled with small pieces, while others have full-bleed images; the colors are vibrant and well-chosen. As a whole, the book succeeds in maintaining dynamic tension, surprising the reader from one spread to the next. It is exquisite and amazingly economical in both design and production.

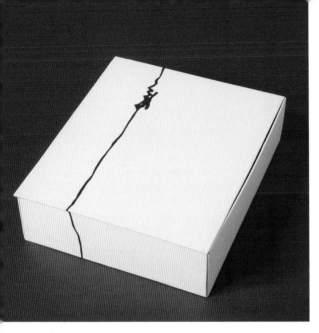

LEFT
The concept for Michelle Kim's portfolio, titled Being Green, springs from the phrase "it's not easy being green." This theme shows the difficulties of being a young designer with much to learn. Since white is a challenging color—and easily soiled—it shows Kim's attention to detail in design and presentation. The red stripe that wraps around the portfolio box represents the struggle and determination of a young designer.

BELOW
To further emphasize the idea of being green and striving for growth, Kim arranged the work chronologically. By the end of the book, it's clear that she's matured in her ability to design and solve problems. In addition, the book's format makes it easy to rearrange items without having to create a new edition.

visual harmony?
the typographic language of herbert bayer & buro destruct

written and designed by michelle j. kim

TOP

Kim's entire portfolio took three days to assemble, including the box and the book. Waiting for materials to ship and printing took longer, so be sure to factor in production time. The total cost of the entire portfolio (box and book) was about $65, because Kim was able to print on the school's equipment for free. The major expenses involved purchasing book cloth, adhesive, and binder's board.

ABOVE

Kim's box opens first to a book and résumé. She uses Cialux Italian book cloth for the binding because it's strong, economical, familiar, and compatible with traditional bookbinding adhesives. The red stripe was also cut from book cloth. Kim's decision to use the same material for the stripe prevents one texture from dominating the other. Underneath the book and résumé, there's a second space hidden by white cloth board where Kim conceals a few original pieces.

LEFT

A recent graduate of Savannah College of Art and Design, Michael Brenner chose a square shape for his portfolio because the physical form intrigued him. He found it much more challenging to work with a square composition than a rectangle or other geometric form. The nine-square grid system gives his portfolio an industrial feel. Because of its rigorous grid, the hard edges of the wooden cover are a perfect complement to the piece.

BELOW

The photographs inside Brenner's book show hands holding the design pieces, giving them both relative scale and a human element. He also offers viewers a better idea of the tactile experience present in his work with the wooden silk-screened cover, which makes each book different.

LIMITED EDITION MAPLE SYRUP
This maple syrup packaging was used as a holiday gift from the Winterhouse studio in 2005. Its vintage was limited to 200 bottles.

Above
Detail of three hang tags designed to accompany maple syrup bottle.

Opposite
Maple syrup bottle in mailing box.

This Page
Detail of closed box with belly band.

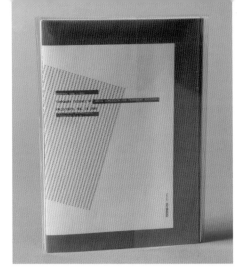

RIGHT and BELOW
Mimi Jung, a Cooper Union graduate and resident of Frankfurt, Germany, designed her student portfolio as a single-page, two-sided poster that she sent in a translucent sleeve, allowing her to make as many copies as she needed.

OPPOSITE
Now that she is out of school, Jung has a portfolio that consists of a collection of individual pieces that are organized to be turned and flipped like the pages of an unbound book, or unfolded into larger, poster-size works. The very last item at the back is a poster, which the viewer is asked to unfold as the climax of the presentation. Because there are no costs for assembling or binding, the overall format is an economical approach to a portfolio that still offers a substantial presentation to art directors.

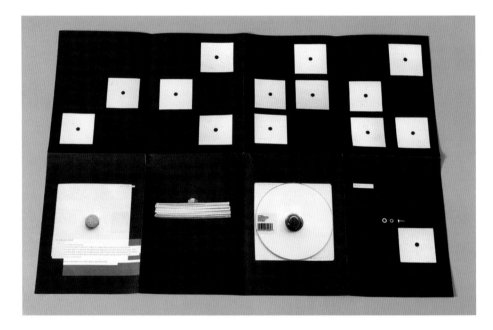

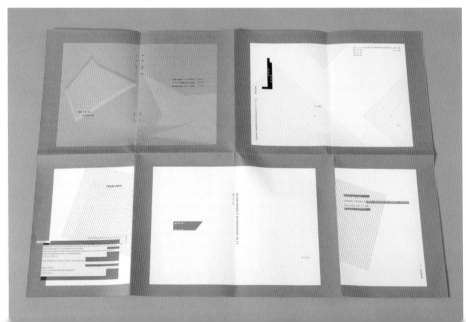

ART BOOKS

THE LESSON

USE ONLY A NO. 2 OR HB PENCIL TO COMPLETE THIS ANSWER
TO EACH QUESTION. DO NOT USE INK. MARK NO MORE THAN ONE ANSWER TO EACH QUESTION.
BE SURE TO FILL IN COMPLETELY THE SPACE FOR YOUR INTENDED MARKABLE CHOICE.
IF YOU ERASE DO SO COMPLETELY. MAKE NO STRAY MARKS.
RIGHT MARK ⬤   WRONG MARKS

THE LESSON IS A REGISTERED TRADEMARK OF THE THEATER BOARD

POSTERS

TEMPORARY EVIDENCE OF LAWFUL ADMISSION FOR PERMANENT RESIDENCE

VALID UNTIL FEB. 28 1995

OPPOSITE, TOP LEFT
Sophie Nicolay, a recent graduate of the Rhode Island
School of Design, has a beautiful cloth-covered custom-
made box for her portfolio. A small picture inset person-
alizes the formal presentation.

OPPOSITE, TOP RIGHT, and BOTTOM
Nicolay created two half-size black inner folders that
fit neatly, side by side, in the top of her portfolio. Each
folder contains a magazine-size book.

BELOW
After the two inner folders are removed and reviewed,
a client or creative director can proceed to a series of
well-trimmed, uniform black boards, each with a different mounted portfolio piece. The order for viewing
the work is clear because there are a limited number
of pieces to be reassembled. The effect of Nicolay's
portfolio is dazzling; it is clean, elegant, and suitable
for corporate clients.

Helen Zhai created this stunning handmade box for her final presentation and portfolio at the Massachusetts College of Art. It features an etched metal piece on the opening edge, and the work inside fits perfectly in the large box. Because many of her student pieces were oversized, this format was necessary. It is exciting and dramatic to see the publication pieces in their original form rather than reduced to a "manageable" size. Zhai keeps the box in a protective cloth carrying case, though the material she chose for the exterior is durable and dark enough to avoid marks or scuffing.

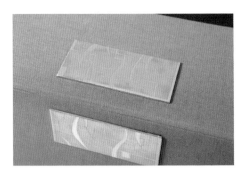

LEFT, BELOW, and OPPOSITE (BELOW)
During the end-of-the-year show at UCLA Design | Media Arts, parts of Roxane Zargham's portfolio were stolen and never returned. This ten-part portfolio she created to replace her former portfolio is both an unbound book and series of posters. Each signature contains an outer layer with explanations and writings on the work and an inside layer showing the work of that particular area or medium. When unfolded and viewed as posters, the portfolio spells out ROXANE 2005.

Hidden in the middle of the portfolio are Zargham's business card and résumé. Both are consistent with the brand, reflecting the central motifs, typography, and colors.

This portfolio, which comes wrapped in a clear plastic sheet, makes the overall presentation accessible, transparent, tactile, and personal. It is a complete design piece that evolves as it reveals chosen objects, immersing the reader in Zargham's work, process, and mind.

Many spreads experiment with simple, classical typography and strong imagery, but the last page of Zargham's portfolio is extremely striking: she printed all the fronts and backs of her portfolio pages on top of one another. In other words, every single page is combined into one single spread at the end of the book. Layer upon layer, photographs, typography, and text come together in a visual collision.

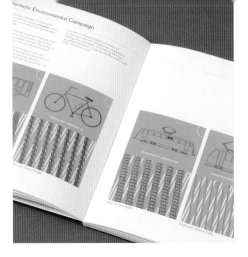

Kathryn Cho's portfolio is a bound book that spans five years of work. It is simple and uniform, allowing the material to take the lead. Cho, a graduate of Cooper Union, uses dots as graphic elements because they reference both print (DPI) and computer screens (pixels).

To enhance the theme, Cho put the book in a bag with a dot pattern to reflect the way that graphic design permeates all mediums (shown opposite). As she says, "That is how I try to approach design: an interdisciplinary approach through multiple disciplines."

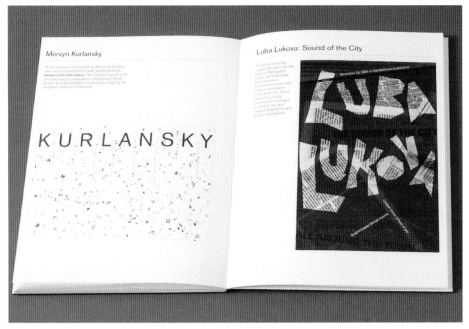

Kathryn Cho
works from 2001 to 2005

Lorenzo Geiger lives in Bern, Switzerland, and Paris, France, where he works at Studio Apeloig. While in school, he created a simple, small, and slender handout portfolio, which contains exquisite pen-and-ink drawings for CDs, labels, and stickers.

HELLO [AGAIN]

HELLO [STRANGER]
HELLO [AGAIN]
HELLO [WORLD]
HELLO [AGAIN]
HELLO [WORLD]

MICROPEPLIDAE

CONTACT [SAY HELLO]

HELLO [AGAIN]

HELLO [AGAIN]

HELLO

CONTACT [SAY HELLO]

Nontraditional Portfolios

How do you define a nontraditional portfolio? The most distinguishing feature is often an unusual exterior—a record box, film can, or vintage suitcase. But some nontraditional portfolios don't have a container at all, as you'll see in this chapter. The only time a nontraditional portfolio is appropriate is when it fits the designer and suits the design need. Don't decide to be different just for the sake of being different. The portfolio should match the work, and never overpower or upstage the design samples inside.

Louise Fili's office is the perfect portfolio, because it's the best way to see her product designs. When you open the door to Louise Fili Ltd, you're greeted by shelves of olive oil, wine, vinegar, cracker tins, and original antique signs and toys. This parade of food packaging, books, and restaurant signs continues into Fili's central office. If a client is willing to pay an office visit, Fili says she is assured of getting the job.

Christian Steurer

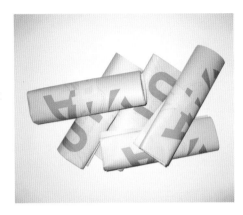

Designer Christian Steurer has worked all over Germany, and in 2001, he printed a newspaper to show his work and write about his personal habits, weaknesses of character, and political thoughts, among other things. The opening pages feature the answers to 250 questions that the designer posed to important associates and family members. As one might expect, the answers reveal a great deal about Steurer.

Though he had no intention of going into newspaper design, the format gave Steurer a way to communicate quickly, simply, and effectively thoughts about his work. As an original design solution, it offered him an edge with employers by allowing his work to stand apart from other designers. He mailed them as newspapers, rolled and sealed with a special sticker that read, "Good designers make trouble."

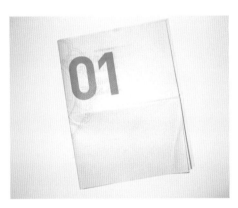

The reaction to Steurer's portfolio was quite positive. Designers from Hamburg, Berlin, and Munich contacted him to talk about design propositions. In addition, the exercise gave him an overview of his work during his first five years as a freelancer. The portfolio also helped him land his current job at Fuenfwerken Design.

The newspaper is printed in offset, in a print run of 600. The colors are black and a fluorescent green on 60 gsm (grams per square meter) paper. As a portfolio, it is unique, well designed, and original.

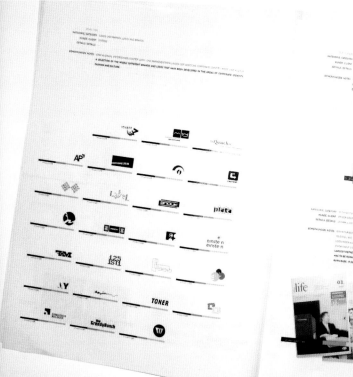

Erin Diebboll

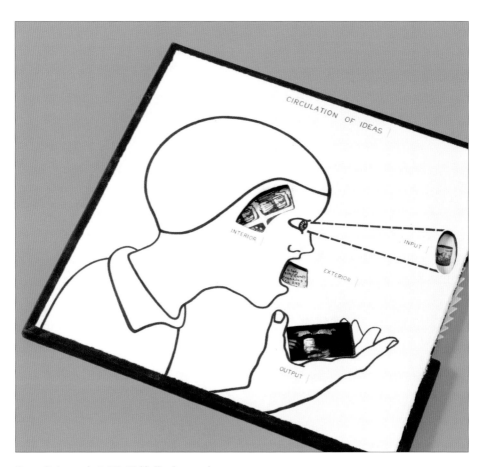

Cooper Union graduate Erin Diebboll's clever sculptural portfolio features a spinning wheel that brings images into view in windows with the following headings: input, interior, exterior, and output. The designer wanted viewers to review her process in relation to the finished art. *Input* is the problem as it is presented to the artist, *interior* shows the artist contemplating the problem visually, *exterior* is the description of the final artwork, and *output* is the artwork itself.

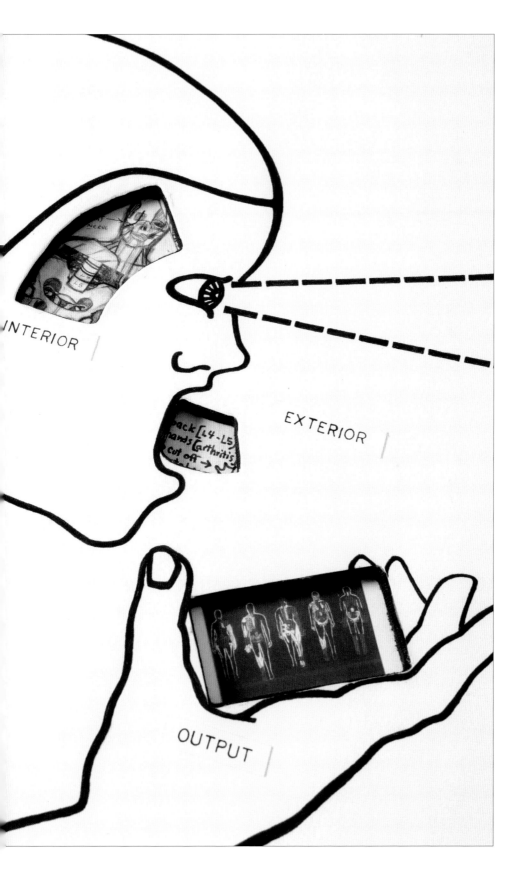

Einat Imber

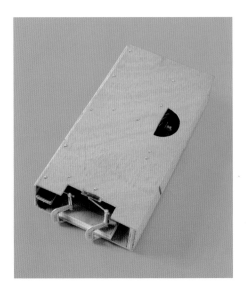

Einat Imber, a recent graduate of Cooper Union, struc-
tured her portfolio to be several books in one, as her
work contains both sculpture and photography. Each
book is a series of photographs with one underlying
concept. The portfolio itself is also a sculpture, and
as an original work it represents her love of three-
dimensional design.

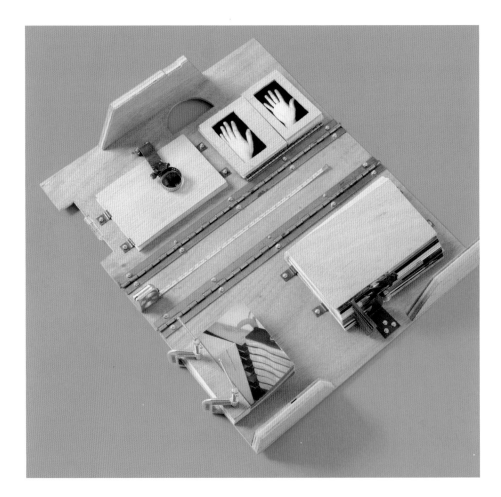

Imber describes her portfolio this way: "I used a flip book for one sculpture that was a moving piece, and I wanted to capture this movement. The overall aesthetic of the book reflects my working space and that's why I used raw materials and different hardware. It was also important for me to keep all the books slightly revealed."

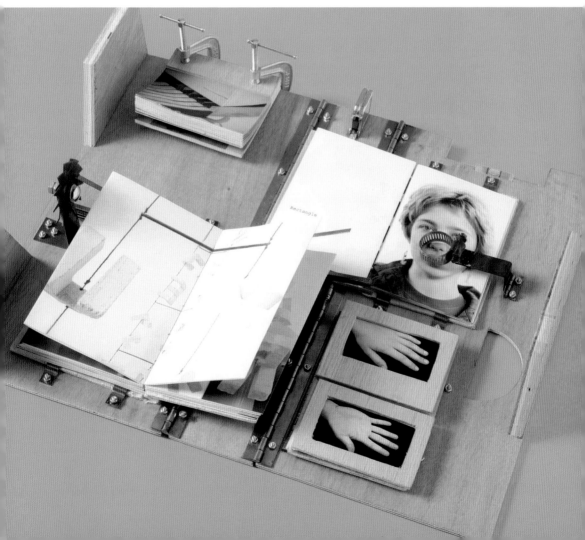

Eramos Tantos

Eramos Tantos, a design studio in Mexico City, sends its portfolio in a film can, which makes a remarkably sturdy portfolio. It also connotes recycling, a nod to the tradition of Mexican folk art in which ordinary things are used in extraordinary new ways. The cardboard packaging (shown at right) around the outside of the canister is covered with the firm's labels and sticker design—a touch that makes the presentation fully consistent.

A small rectangular book is neatly secured in a felt form, preventing it from shifting in transit and getting damaged. The book itself is a ring binder with samples printed in-house, meaning that it can be replaced or refreshed at any time.

Nathan Zarse

Nathan Zarse, a recent graduate of Herron School of Art
and Design, carries a vintage suitcase as his portfolio
case, which is consistent with his interest in reviving
1940s and 1950s design styles. It opens to reveal a
group of ordinary manila envelopes—affixed with his
distinctive label—along with one antique leatherette
notebook.

RIGHT
Inside one of the envelopes is a book. When Zarse presents his portfolio, he opens the book to the title page of an essay, "4 Arguments for the Elimination of Television." The page features a grainy TV screen as a visual complement to the message. Any portfolio piece that takes a stand on an issue, or poses and then answers a question, helps an art director understand the person behind the work and their interests.

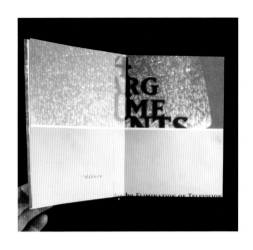

ABOVE
A second page from the book speaks of television as part of an artificial environment and likens the human experience to an astronaut being cut loose from his lifelines.

Another envelope reveals a group of brochures on various subjects. The individual manila envelopes give Zarse a method for grouping his materials. They are economical and easily replaced, and they fit with the old suitcase stylistically. The portfolio is clever; it's unified, economical, and thoughtful.

Kevin O'Callaghan

Kevin O'Callaghan teaches 3-D design and illustration at the School of Visual Arts in New York City. He encourages his students to design beyond two dimensions by manipulating found objects to create meaning. The story of his giant portfolio is legendary. He built and hauled a 15' (4.6 m)-tall portfolio on a trailer behind his car to Milton Glaser's office, only to have it lodge under a bridge. After some hasty adjustments to the air in his tires, he arrived fifty minutes late to the interview. Glaser asked to see the portfolio and was brought to the window to peer at the giant portfolio three stories below. O'Callaghan was forgiven for being late, and his career was launched when Glaser made several calls to recommend him.

Chris Dimino

A student of O'Callaghan, Chris Dimino began his portfolio with a simple cube because he felt it was a fitting way to exhibit three-dimensional work. He settled on a shape big enough to hold 4" × 5" (10.2 × 12.7 cm) chromes, then experimented a lot with card-board models and considered how to open the box without damaging it. The result is a remarkable piece that even after being out of school for three years, Dimino still takes to interviews because "it carries an impact that simply does not come from the traditional portfolio book." He adds, "When I bring the cube I know that I am about to show an interviewer something that they have never seen before. And to me that means a lot, considering the design competition of New York City." (He also has a regular 8.5" × 11" (21.6 × 27.9 cm) book for his newer work.

ABOVE and OPPOSITE (TOP)
Dimino's case opens by lightly pressing on and turning the top handle. When the top is pulled back, the interior reveals a small light box standing on end and two sym-metrical compartments for the chrome photographs. After a brief setup, the viewer removes each chrome from the left side pocket, places it on the light box in the middle for viewing, then moves it to the right side pocket when finished.

OPPOSITE (MIDDLE and BOTTOM)
"In fabricating the case, I was fortunate that my father worked at the Long Island Railroad at the time," says Dimino. "Although I was not able to use their machin-ery due to union rules, I was able to work at the side of a tinsmith to carry out my design. Even though I had the design thoroughly planned out, we still ran into some problems along the way. By the end of the fabrication, we had drawn the interest of the whole shop crew, who were throwing out suggestions on any sort of problem we came across."

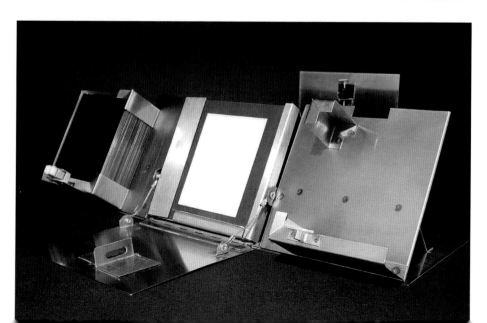

In addition to a strong presentation, the success of Dimino's portfolio rests on solid design work. One striking sample is a photo of a piece that was featured in an exhibit with O'Callaghan called The Next Best . . . Ding! Given a typewriter as a starting point, Dimino had to give new life to this obsolete object. One of his solutions: turn it into a vacuum cleaner, merging the typewriter's casing with a vacuum cleaner from the same time period.

Most of the projects in O'Callaghan's class push the limits of conceptual, as well as mechanical, ability. The work in Dimino's cube ranges from conceptual and product design to set design and model making. This diversity makes for a great portfolio.

Margaux Frankel

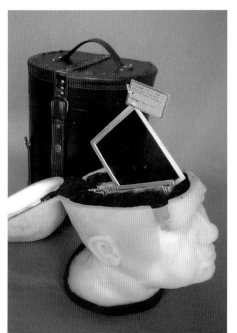

Margaux Frankel also studied with O'Callaghan. For her portfolio, she produced a cast of her own head that is hinged at the top to reveal slides. She found that the reactions were so positive that she became known worldwide as the girl with the head portfolio. "I have taken the head on many an interview, and it always gets interesting reactions," she says. "I bring it because it shows my creativity and ability to think outside the box in addition to showing a little humor in my design."

Boworndej Wangkeo

Boworndej Wangkeo converted an old picture book into a conceptual portfolio. It opens to reveal a slide projector and images of works created in O'Callaghan's 3-D class. The principle behind all the items in the portfolio is finding good ways to reconsider and reassign meaning to everyday objects around us. The first image shows a multipurpose lunchbox that doubles as a board game.

RIGHT
One of the slides in Wangkeo's portfolio shows this moon man golf-swing trainer. It's his response to an assignment that challenged him to find an active use for a product that is usually inactive. In this case the inactive object was an MTV music trophy. By turning it into a game, Wangkeo gave the trophy a new use.

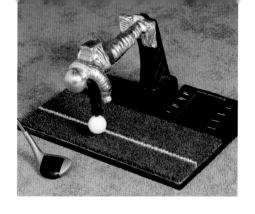

ABOVE
Another slide in Wangkeo's portfolio shows these Mona Lisa chairs that he designed for a theme restaurant. Like images on a website, slides allow a designer to show objects that aren't portable and to unify a physically mismatched group of items.

RIGHT
Wangkeo's Plexiglas stop sign was the response to this assignment: Render a product useless by changing the design or materials with which it was originally made. As with the other entries in Wangkeo's portfolio, this piece shows his ability to challenge traditional meaning in the symbols around us and to think creatively beyond two dimensions.

Kristie Downing

With the goal of working in the recording industry after graduating from Massachusetts College of Art, Kristie Downing, now a designer at VSA Partners in Chicago, chose a vintage record box for her first portfolio. Inside the box, simple vinyl sleeves hold various designs, such as *Harvard Design Magazine*, résumés, and a type broadside advertising music lessons. There's also a simple ring holding various calling card designs and a mini-portfolio featuring reduced samples of recent work. The overall effect is a unique box full of wonderful samples that makes a bold statement.

Downing's first résumé was silk-screened on a 45 rpm record sleeve (containing an actual record), which listed her curriculum vitae, internship information, and various awards. A business card bears the motto "Design without soul is life without passion." All the pieces fit nicely into a vellum envelope. While Downing never worked in the recording industry, her portfolio succeeded in catching the attention of some of her biggest design heroes.

Interactive Portfolios and Websites

Websites are broad and international in reach. A website is inclusive and anonymous; anyone with an Internet connection can visit a site without the designer or firm knowing who he or she is. It is also available at all hours of the day and night in many locations around the world. Because of this, a well-designed website is a great vehicle for showing both a designer's style and areas of expertise. Designers and design studios frequently contract with website designers or technicians to design their sites, and collaborate closely on the organization and development.

Amber Frid-Jimenez
web.media.mit.edu/~amber/

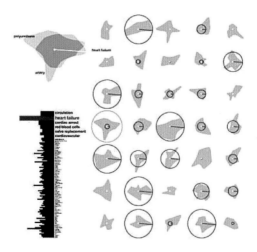

Amber Frid-Jimenez
Work | Cognitive Machines | Document Icons

Deb Roy, Philip DeCamp, Amber Frid-Jimenez

< > 1 2 3 **4**

Document Icons
Software designed to allow the user to search intuitively through content of seven million text documents by reconfiguring histograms used by common search engines.

A. We begin with a histogram of words and their corresponding weights relative to a given set of documents. We order the histogram to form loosely defined concepts.

B. We wrap the histogram data around a point and draw bounding boxes to define salient concept areas. We then create a shape which becomes the documents profile showing comparing concept areas within the document.

C. The interface shows the document icons as they would be used to compare between 30-100 documents in a single frame.

Amber Frid-Jimenez studies with John Maeda in the Physical Language Workshop at the MIT Media Lab in Cambridge, Maassachsetts. This page from her website displays one of her many designs under the heading Cognitive Machines. The simplicity of the layout is a perfect complement to the complexity of the work being shown.

Amber Frid-Jimenez
Work | Cognitive Machines | Semantic Landscape

< > 1 2 **3** 4

Deb Roy, Philip DeCamp, Amber Frid-Jimenez

Semantic Landscape
Marc Weeber's paper on "Developing a
Test Collection for Biomedical Word Sense
Disambiguation" gives the following three
senses of the term "cold": 1) temperature
indication, 2) the acronym for Chronic
Obstructive Lung Disease, and 3) a
common disease. The semantic landscape
at right investigates this example of sense
disambiguation among US Patent
documents.

3. This visualization shows the overall
terrain from the perpectival viewpoint.

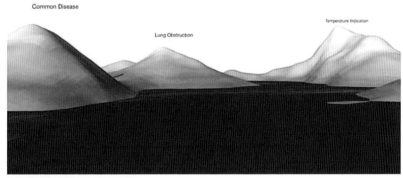

Semantic terrain from the groundplane viewpoint

Jimenez's site clearly illustrates how she makes visual representations of complex
ideas and theories. Her easy-to-navigate design, using primarily black, gray, and red,
allows the user to pick from a row of options, each of which shifts from gray to red
when that option is chosen.

Amber Frid-Jimenez
web.media.mit.edu/~amber/

Amber Frid-Jimenez
Work | Cognitive Machines | Document Icons

Deb Roy, Philip DeCamp, Amber Frid-Jimenez

< > **1** 2 3 4

Document Icons
Software designed to allow the user to
search intuitively through content of seven
million text documents by reconfiguring
histograms used by common search
engines.

A. We begin with a histogram of words and
their corresponding weights relative to a
given set of documents. We order the
histogram to form loosely defined
concepts.

B. We wrap the histogram data around a
point and draw bounding boxes to define
salient concept areas. We then create a
shape which becomes the documents
profile showing comparing concept areas
within the document.

C. The interface shows the document icons
as they would be used to compare between
30-100 documents in a single frame.

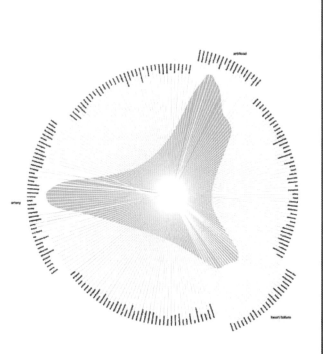

Another page from the cognitive section of Jimenez's website shows how histograms
gather information to form loosely defined concepts. Here, Jimenez again has constructed rotating three-dimensional graphics to help the viewer visualize the idea.

Amber Frid-Jimenez
Work | Computation

< > 1 2 3 4 5 6 **7**

Preludes
screenshots from interactive program, 2004

The program reconstructs T.S. Flint's
Preludes.

aAaaa
That fade behind a city block
all all.
The worlds revolve like ancient women
You dozed, and watched the night revealing
And the light crept up between the shutters
And short square fingers stuffing pipes,
I am moved by fancies that are curled
And at the corner of the street
Of faint stale smells of beer
The conscience of a blackened street
On trampled by insistent feet
To early coffee-stands.

Of which your soul was constituted;
The burnt-out ends of smoky days.
dozed early edge-ends evening
And evening newspapers, and eyes
feet feet fingers-five.
And newspapers from vacant lots;
You curled the papers from your hair,
The notion of some infinitely gentle
You curled the papers from your hair,
And you heard the sparrows in the gutters,

Around these images, and cling
Gathering fuel in vacant lots
lay leaves, light lighting like lonely lots
With the other masquerades
And newspapers from vacant lots;
At four and five and six o'clock
And then the lighting of the lamps.
On broken blinds and chimney-pots,
And short square fingers stuffing pipes,
That are raising dingy shades
scraps settles shades short shower;
The showers beat
The burnt-out ends of smoky days.
A lonely cab-horse steams and stamps

On this Web page, Jimenez interprets T. S. Eliot's poem "Preludes" typographically
by alternating highly legible with totally illegible type.

Louise Fili LTD
www.louisefili.com

Louise Fili's website is spare yet perfectly matched to her designs. The site opens
with the initials of her company name, LFL (top). The letters unfold onto the screen
and elegantly fade back to gray as smaller type outlining her specialty appears in the
forefront (above). A simple rollover identification system immediately offers several
options that allow for easy navigation, and from any place on the site, returning to
the main menu is intuitive and foolproof. The photography is simple and consistent,
and the overall site is well designed.

One section of Fili's site is dedicated to her food-packaging designs. In a traditional print presentation, segues between cracker tins (top), margarita mixes and salts (above), logos, and restaurant signs would be awkward, but on a website, these transitions become seamless, and the designs hold together perfectly.

Louise Fili LTD
www.louisefili.com

In these three examples, Fili shows her logos and restaurant signs against an elegant white background. The name of the client appears in small type above the image.

Skolos-Wedell
www. skolos-wedell.com

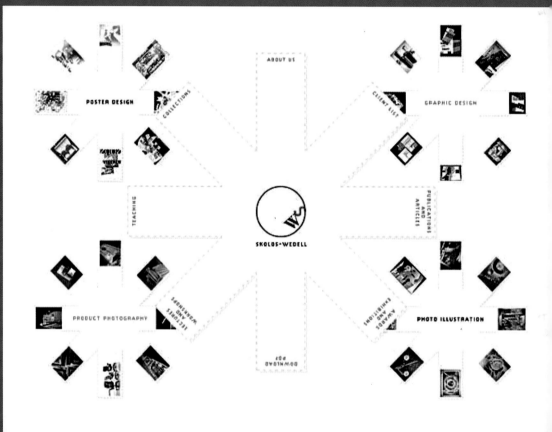

Skolos-Wedell's website is very engaging. While it loads, spinning roulette wheels roll onto the page (above). Each wheel has eight thumbnail tabs that feature work from the area the wheel represents, such as poster design, product photography, graphic design, and photo illustration. After these images have loaded, a fifth wheel containing general categories such as awards, clients, contact information, teaching, and lectures spins into the center.

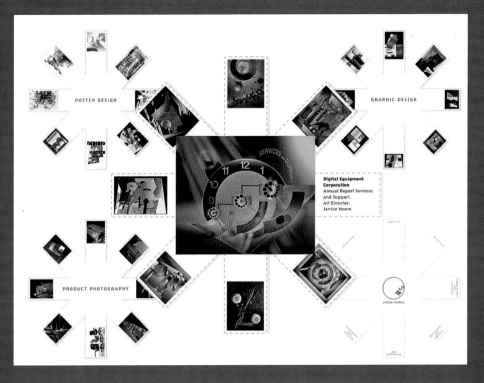

One of the most exciting things about this website is the format—its kinetic nature differentiates the site from the vertical and horizontal grids that dominate the Web. And since there are no layers or subcategories, viewers never get lost. Users simply click on a thumbnail option to cause the subject to spin into the forefront and open. The purity of the design gives it a certain strength.

Eramos Tantos
www.eramostantos.com

The design studio Eramos Tantos of Mexico City features all of the website's content on what almost looks like a distressed piece of paper tacked on the dark red background. Although a large variety of the firm's design work is shown, only the content in this central area varies, as demonstrated in these three examples.

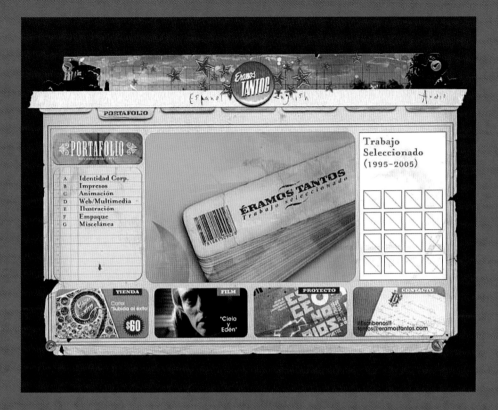

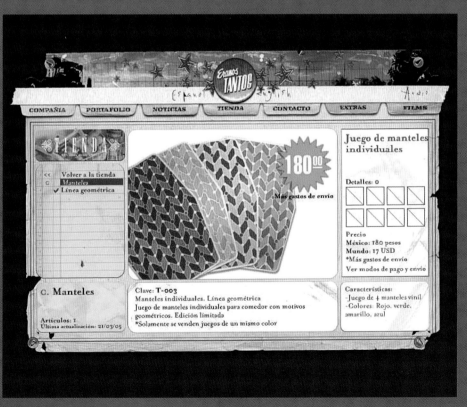

Eramos Tantos
www.eramostantos.com

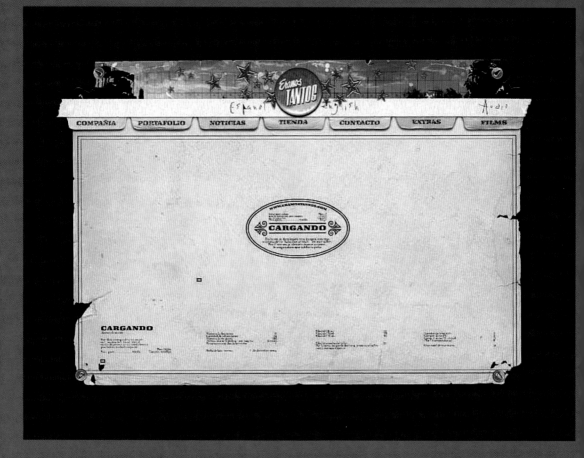

In Mexico, found objects and recycled materials have become part of folk art. The firm's website borrows type and other ideas from old cigar boxes, tickets, and found items, and thus celebrates both the Mexican vernacular and its folk tradition.

Mayo Bucher
www.mayobucher.com

Mayo Bucher, a talented Swiss graphic designer and painter, uses this simple splash page (top) to promote his work. It makes the most of his unusual name and offers three options at the bottom of the screen: English, email, and Deutsch. Once you choose either the English or German version of the site, completely unadorned typography offers you a route to paintings or architecture.

Bucher's work covers everything from paintings and installations to architecture and photomontage—all of which are well displayed on his website. The site is easy to navigate, and the images are bold and simply placed.

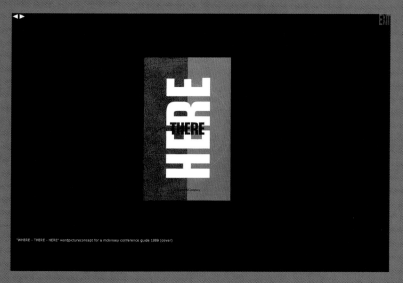

"WHERE - THERE - HERE" wordpictureconcept for a mckinsey conference guide 1999 (cover)

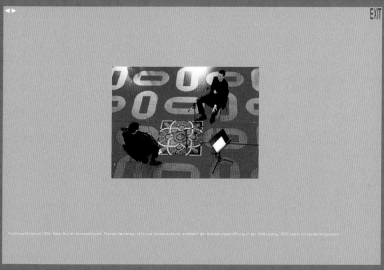

Poetryperformance 1234, Havo Bücher Konzept/Notäsk, Thomas Demenga, Cello und Computersound, entwickelt bei der Ausstellungseröffnung an der HGB Leipzig, 2002 (www.thomasdemenga.com)

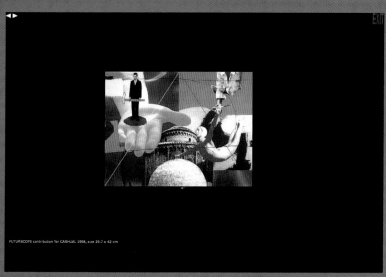

FUTURSCOPE contribution for CASHUAL 1998, size 29.7 x 42 cm

Mike Essl
www.essl.com

Mike Essl is a highly talented Web designer and teacher at Cooper Union. His website promises, "If I say it enough, you will believe that I am the greatest." From this splash page, the viewer selects works that will be displayed on the left from a candy box of posters on the right. Because the viewer can see so many thumbnails at once, Essl's enormous range yet surprising consistency quickly becomes evident.

The site is simple to navigate and lets the design work speak for itself. Clicking on one thumbnail reveals a typeface Essl designed after he gave a lecture at Grand Valley State University in Michigan, where he was taken to a bar called Teazers. He says the sign was made from what looked like picket fence materials. "After I got back to Cranbrook [Academy of Art], I took those forms and made a new typeface."

Mike Essl
www.essl.com

This poster on Essl's site announces a lecture given by Modern Dog at Cranbrook (above). The piece features a shadow puppet dog and a corn dog all carefully composed and cropped into a design. The vibrant colors and images reproduce better on the screen than they would in print, and because Essl is primarily a website designer, he prefers to show his work in this format.

Weirdo Deluxe is a book Essl designed with Brian Romero (opposite, top). His idea was "a simple one—design an art book that doesn't retreat from the art. Even the most beautiful art books are often times very quiet. Minimal typography is employed to create a design voice that never speaks louder than the voice of the artist. Lowbrow art, on other hand, is very lush, often screaming for your attention. The cover of the book was inspired by the Fruity Pebbles logo."

The image shown opposite, bottom, shows a timeline from *Weirdo Deluxe*. Essl represented each era as a Candyland-style board game, with a different color for each year.

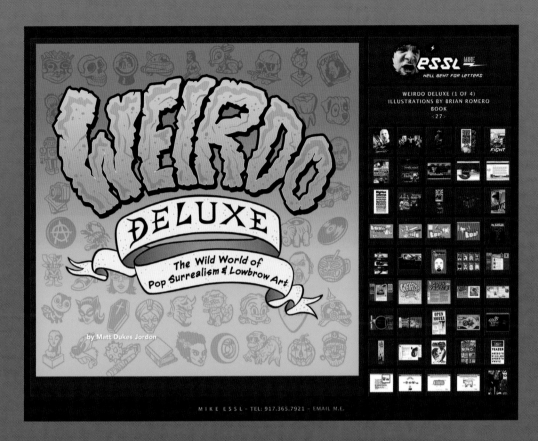

Melle Hammer
www.mellehammer.nl

March 17 1956 | Melle Hammer ...it's a boy!

Typographer. Designer. Teacher.
Lingering between art, design and advertising.
Easily seduced to design a table, a chair or a stage-set.
Every now and then a movie or a poem comes out.
Always questioning the spot.
On and on surprised, outraged or in love. Lost?
Found!

mH, Amsterdam +31(0)20 623 97 02
xc2me@xs4all.nl

Click anywhere to meet an

Melle Hammer of the Netherlands has a website that opens with an image of himself and text describing his passion for design, poetry, and theater design (shown above, top). Users simply click anywhere on the page to see more work. The website transcends simple advertisement by describing Hammer as a typographer, designer, and teacher "lingering between art design and advertising" and "easily seduced to design a table, a chair, or a stage. Every now and then, a movie or a poem comes out."

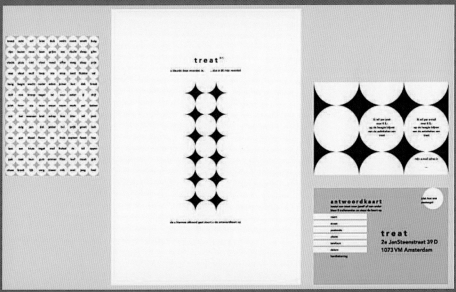

To navigate the site, the user is asked to click anywhere on the opening page. An additional window is launched, which may feature any number of things including pictures of himself in performance art, a series of tickets he designed, or a small puppet theater he created for the streets of the Hague, (opposite, bottom and this page). With the diversity of Hammer's creative interests, a website is the perfect format for him to show his seemingly unrelated work in a cohesive presentation.

PART III

Resources

Portfolio Suppliers

Kolo
Kolo, LLC
P.O. Box 572
Windsor, CT 06095-0572 USA
888.636.5656
www.kolo.com

Prat Portfolios
Prat/Paris Inc.
4340 Almaden Expressway, #210
San Jose, CA 95118 USA
800.900.4720
www.prat.com

Pina Zangaro
2200 Jerrold Avenue
Unit L
San Francisco, CA 94124 USA
415.206.9582
www.pinazangaro.com

Contributors

American Institute of Graphic Arts
164 Fifth Avenue
New York, NY 10010 USA
212.807.1990
www.aiga.org

Judith Aronson
Simmons College
300 The Fenway
Boston, MA 02115 USA
617.354.7887
aronsonj@simmons.edu

Hyun Auh
42-25 Layton St. #1B
Elmhurst, NY 11373 USA
646.644.7665
auhdesign@yahoo.com

Kobi Benezri
I.D. Magazine
38 East 29th Street, Floor 3
New York, NY 10014 USA
212.447.1400 ext. 132
kobi.benezri@id-mag.com

Milan Bozic
49 Bogart Street #34
Brooklyn, NY 11206 USA
732.207.0455
londoncalled@cs.com

Michael William Brenner
23 Reservoir Road
Lakeville, CT 06039 USA
860.485.5044
mwbrenner@mac.com

Mayo Bucher
Hottingerstrasse 28
CH-8032 Zurich, Switzerland
41.1252.0096
mail@mayobucher.com
www.mayobucher.com

Chermayeff & Geismar Studio
15 East 26th Street, 12th floor
New York, NY 10010 USA
212.532.4595
www.cgstudionyc.com

Kathryn Cho
Astoria, NY 11102-4030 USA
718.354.0749
kathryn.cho@gmail.com

Mats Dahle
BRGFX (Bergen Graphics)
Olav Kyrres Gate 39
5005 Bergen, Norway
47.9.5186.377
mats@brgfx.com

Erin Diebboll
25 Hillside Road
Lincoln, MA 01773 USA
646.483.8192
ediebboll@yahoo.com

Chris Dimino
516.652.8795
cdimino@designhead.net
www.designhead.net/cdimino

Kristie Downing
kristie@synapsetosynapse.com

Jim Drobka
3106 Berkeley Circle
Los Angeles, CA 90026 USA
323.665.5523
drobka@getty.edu

Eramos Tantos
Suiza 16
Portales 03300
Mexico City, Mexico
52.55.56.74.15.16
tantos@eramostantos.com

Mike Essl
366 Sackett Street
Brooklyn, NY 11231 USA
917.365.7921
mike@essl.com
www.essl.com

Margaux Frankel
14 Patricia Lane
Cos Cob, CT 06807 USA
203.536.3834
mlfran@aol.com

Amber Frid-Jimenez
354 Congress Street
Boston, MA 02210 USA
617.399.0791
amber@media.mit.edu
web.media.mit.edu/~amber/

Geoffry Fried
The Art Institute of Boston at Lesley University
700 Beacon Street
Boston, MA 02215 USA
gfried@aiboston.edu

Lorenzo Geiger
Muristrasse 67
CH-3006 Bern, Switzerland
41.0.76.443.97.97
ted@biwak.net
www.biwak.net

Green Dragon Office
948 Muirfield Road
Los Angeles, CA 90019 USA
323.549.4288
www.greendragonoffice.com

Hansje van Halem, graphic design
Berberisstraat 16
1032 EL Amsterdam, Netherlands
31.6.412.415.46
hansje@hansje.net

Melle Hammer
NEW Uilenburgerstraat 3E
1001 LM Amsterdam, Netherlands
31.0.20.623.97.02
xc2me@xs4all.nl
www.mellehammer.nl

Sagi Haviv
250 West 19th Street #14D
New York, NY 10011 USA
917.538.9114
sagihaviv@yahoo.com

Crista Hirzel
Oescherstrasse 25
8702 Zollikon, Switzerland
41.1.391.5016
chirzel@attglobal.net

Holly Horner
65 Rusthall Avenue
London W4 1BN UK
44.781.0605.975
hollyhorner2@hotmail.com

Einat Imber
136 McKibbin Street, #16
Brooklyn, NY 11206 USA
718.302.5698
eina_tz@yahoo.com

Mimi Jung
Bruckenstrasse 13
60594 Frankfurt am Main, Germany
49.163.46.96.218
mimijung914@yahoo.com

Chip Kidd
315 East 68th Street PH-E
New York, NY 10021 USA
212.572.2363
ckidd@randomhouse.com

Michelle Kim
3826 North Tazewell Street
Arlington, VA 22207 USA
571.243.5237
mjk8a@hotmail.com

Hirokazu Kurebayashi
2 17 28, Shibazaki-cho Tachikawa-shi
Tokyo 190-0023, Japan
81.42.522.2247
hirokazu_kurebayashi@yahoo.co.jp

Peter Lehman
WGBH
125 Western Avenue
Boston, MA 02134 USA
617.300.4016
peter_lehman@wgbh.org

LOGO
San Salvador 2022
11200, Montevideo, Uruguay
598.2.411.3376
logo@montevideo.com.uy

Louise Fili Ltd
156 Fifth Avenue, Suite 925
New York, NY 10010 USA
212.989.9153
louise@louisefili.com
www.louisefili.com

Robin Lynch
Negerkunst Studio
45 Southgate Avenue
Hastings on Hudson, NY 10706 USA
914.674.9111
negerkunst@aol.com

Rebeca Mendez
Rebeca Mendez Communication Design
2873 North Mount Curve Avenue
Altadena, CA 91001 USA
626.794.1334
balam@earthlink.net

Margaret Morton
The Cooper Union
30 Cooper Square
New York, NY 10003 USA
212.353-4208
www.fragiledwelling.org

Sophie Nicolay
270 Gano Street
Providence, RI 02906 USA

Deborah Norcross
9 Travis Road
Natick, MA 01760 USA
508.653.7492
dnorcross@mac.com

Kevin O'Callaghan
49 Shore Road
Stony Brook, NY 11790 USA
212.592.2163
ocaldesign@yahoo.com

Janet Odgis
Odgis + Company
51 East 42nd Street, Suite 1205
New York, NY 10017 USA
212.286.0277
odgis@odgis.com
www.odgis.com

Chris Pullman
WGBH
125 Western Avenue
Boston, MA 02134 USA
617.300.2505
chris_pullman@wgbh.org

Robynne Raye
Modern Dog Design Co.
7903 Greenwood Avenue North
Seattle, WA 98103 USA
206.789.7667
bubbles@moderndog.com
www.moderndog.com

Elizabeth Resnick
Massachusetts College of Art
621 Huntington Avenue
Boston, MA 02115 USA
617.879.7651
ElizRes@massart.edu

George Restrepo
Rest + Design
57 Whiton Avenue
Quincy, MA 02169 USA
617.328.7478
george@rest-design.com
www.rest-design.com

Brian Roettinger
Hand Held Heart
4318 Los Feliz Boulevard, #7
Los Angeles, CA 90027 USA
661.607.1735
brian@handheldheart.com
www.handheldheart.com

Louise Sandhaus
California Institute of the Arts
24700 McBean Parkway
Valencia, CA 91355 USA
661.222.2766
sandhaus@calarts.edu
design.calarts.edu

Doug Scott
WGBH
114 Western Avenue
Boston, MA 02134 USA
doug_scott@wgbh.org

Skolos-Wedell
125 Green Street
Canton, MA 02021 USA
781.828.0280
www.skolos-wedell.com

Paul Souza
300 Marion Avenue
Mill Valley, CA 94941 USA
415.381.5500
paul@perfectdesignsense.com
www.perfectdesignsense.com

Will Staehle
lonewolf/blacksheep
9 Valhalla Place
Valhalla, NY 10595 USA
914.374.8103
info@lonewolfblacksheep.com
www.lonewolfblacksheep.com

Christian Steurer
VIA01
Lanzstrasse 3
D-65183 Wiesbaden, Germany
49.611.580.27.39
49.611.580.27.46
christian.steurer@fuenfwerken.com
www.fuenfwerken.com

Stoltze Design
49 Melcher Street, 4th Floor
Boston, MA 02210 USA
617.350.7109
www.stoltzedesign.com

Thonik
Weesperzijde 79d
1091 EJ Amsterdam, Netherlands
31.20.468.3525
studio@thonik.nl
www.thonik.nl

Two Twelve Associates
902 Broadway, 20th Floor
New York, NY 10010 USA

Roberto de Vicq de Cumptich
RVC
1326 Madison Ave., Apt. 31
New York, NY 10128 USA
212.207.7014
roberto.devicq@harpercollins.com

Lucas Walker
228 Springvale Avenue
Everett, MA 02149 USA
978.549.6025
krazywis@yahoo.com

Min Wang
China Central Academy of Fine Arts,
School of Design
No. 8 Hua Jia Di Nan Jie, Chao Yang District
Beijing 100102, China
86.1350.1084.543
mwang@square2.com

Boworndej Wangkeo
10 Nimitz Road
Yonkers, NY 10710 USA
917.664.7871
Bowangkeo@hotmail.com

Wieden + Kennedy Tokyo
7-5-6 Roppongi
Minato-Ku
Tokyo 106-0032, Japan
81.0.3.5771.2900
cruz@wk.com

Andrew Yoon
Jianguo Dong Road, Lane 328
Building 20, Room 1202
Shanghai 200025, China
86.21.134.8274.7111
and
750 Forest Green Drive
La Canada, CA 91011
323.804.1641
me@andrewyoon.com
www.andrewyoon.com

Deenie Yudell
Design Manager, Getty Publications
1200 Getty Center Drive, Suite 500
Los Angeles, CA 90049-1682 USA
dyudell@getty.edu

Roxane Zargham
2038 Fairburn Avenue
Los Angeles, CA 90025 USA
310.474.1239
roxanezargham@yahoo.com

Nathan Zarse
6013 North Pine Grove Avenue, #324
Chicago, IL 60613 USA
317.294.4108
zo3nathan@aol.com
www.nathanzarse.com

Huanwu Zhai
17 McBride Street, #2
Jamaica Plain, MA 02130 USA
617.306.3209
yayazhai@yahoo.com

Chen Zhengda Graphic Design
Zhijiang Hua Yuan
No.7 Zhi Ping Road
Binjiang Zone
310053 Hangzhou, China
86.0571.86696812
zhengda@chenzhengda.com
www.chenzhengda.com

Index

About the Author

Sara Eisenman began her career designing books at Random House for Pantheon, Knopf, and the Modern Library. In 1984, she was appointed Art Director for Alfred A. Knopf jackets. Upon leaving New York City in 1987, she was appointed Art Director of trade and reference jackets and covers at Houghton Mifflin Company. In 1993, she became Creative Director at Beacon Press, where she art-directed and designed book interiors, jackets, and everything book-related for eleven years.

Eisenman continues to teach and design a wide variety of materials and has received design awards from the AIGA (American Institute of Graphic Arts), the American Association of University Publishers, the Society of Illustrators, *Print*, the Art Directors Club, and many others. She has taught at Harvard University, Columbia University Publishing Course, the Radcliffe Publishing Course, and Rhode Island School of Design. She has lectured at Stanford, Harvard, and Columbia Universities and at meetings of the American Association of University Presses. She lives in Milton, Massachusetts.

Acknowledgments

I am particularly grateful to the following people, who have helped me find so many designers and amazing portfolios: Nancy Skolos and Tom Wedell, Margaret Morton, Janet Odgis, Rebeca Mendez, Louise Fili, Adrien Pelletier, Melle Hammer, Kyle Cooper, Chris Pullman, Deenie Yudell, Mimi Jung, Andrew Yoon, Lorraine Wild, Min Wang, Clive Challis, Isaac Tobin, Patricia Duque Campos, and Elizabeth Resnick. A special thanks to Alvin Eisenman and David Godine, who cheered me on with their support and ideas. I'd also like to thank my editor, Kristin Ellison, who invented the idea of this book and offered me the opportunity to be a writer.